Coin Collecting Bible

10 Books in 1

The #1 Guide from Beginners to Advanced to Easily Identify, Value, Preserve Your Collection and Turn Out Your Hobby in a Money Machine!

PETER WILLIAMS

© Copyright 2023 - All rights reserved.

The content contained within this book may not be reproduced, duplicated or transmitted without direct written permission from the author or the publisher. Under no circumstances will any blame or legal responsibility be held against the publisher, or author, for any damages, reparation, or monetary loss due to the information contained within this book. Either directly or indirectly.

Legal Notice:

This book is copyright protected. This book is only for personal use. You cannot amend, distribute, sell, use, quote or paraphrase any part, or the content within this book, without the consent of the author or publisher.

Disclaimer Notice:

Please note the information contained within this document is for educational and entertainment purposes only. All effort has been executed to present accurate, up to date, and reliable, complete information. No warranties of any kind are declared or implied. Readers acknowledge that the author is not engaging in the rendering of legal, financial, medical or professional advice. The content within this book has been derived from various sources. Please consult a licensed professional before attempting any techniques outlined in this book.

By reading this document, the reader agrees that under no circumstances is the author responsible for any losses, direct or indirect, which are incurred as a result of the use of information contained within this document, including, but not limited to, errors, omissions, or inaccuracies

Contents

Introduction 15

Book 1: The Basics Of Coin Collecting 16

    Chapter 1: What Is Coin Collecting? 17

    Chapter 2: Who Collects Coins? 17

        History buffs 18

        Investors 18

        Art enthusiasts 18

        Hobbyists 19

        Inheritors 19

    Chapter 3: The Benefits And Joys Of Coin Collecting 21

        Learning about history and culture 21

        Appreciating the artistry of coins: 22

        Social interaction: 22

        Historical significance: 23

        Challenge and excitement: 23

    Chapter 4: Types Of Coins To Collect 24

        Historical coins: 25

        Rare coins: 25

        Error coins: 26

        Proof coins: 26

Bullion coins: 27

Commemorative coins: 27

Foreign coins: 28

Coin sets: 28

Chapter 5: Essential Numismatic Terms 30

Alloy: 30

American Numismatic Association (ANA): 30

Annealing: 31

Assay: 31

Bag Mark: 31

Bi-Metallic: 31

Blank: 31

Bullion: 32

Business Strike: 32

Bust: 32

Clad Coinage: 32

Collar: 33

Condition: 33

Counterfeit: 33

Currency: 33

Denomination: 33

Die: 34

Edge: 34

Engraver: 34

Error: 34

Face Value: 34

Field: 35

Grade: 35

Hairlines: 35

Incuse: 35

Ingot: 35

Inscription: 36

Intrinsic Value (Bullion Value): 36

Key Date: 36

Legal Tender: 36

Legend: 36

Medal: 36

Medium of Exchange: 37

Mint Luster: 37

Mint Mark: 37

Mint State: 37

Motto: 37

Mylar: 38

Numismatics: 38

Obsolete: 38

Obverse: 38

Off-Center: 38

Overstrike: 38

Pattern: 39

Planchet: 39

Proof Set: 39

Relief: 39

Restrike: 39

Reverse: 39

Riddler: 40

Rim: 40

Roll: 40

Series: 40

Slab: 40

Strike: 40

Type Set: 41

Uncirculated: 41

Upsetting Mill: 41

Variety: 41

Book 2: Evaluating Coin Value 42

Chapter 1: How To Determine A Coin's Worth 43

Research: 43

Assess condition: 43

Check rarity: 43

Consider demand: 44

Consult experts: 44

Chapter 2: The Role Of Grading In Coin Value 45

Chapter 3: A Guide To Understanding Coin Values 46

Rarity: 46

Mintage: 46

Survival rate: 47

Varieties and errors: 47

Historical significance: 48

Condition: 49

Demand: 49

Book 3: Avoiding Forgeries And Counterfeits 51

Chapter 1: Understanding Fake And Counterfeit Coins 52

Counterfeit coins: 52

Altered coins: 52

Polished or cleaned coins: 53

Counter-stamped coins: 54

Replicas: 55

Chapter 2: How To Identify A Forged Coin 56

Weight and size: 56

Edge lettering: 57

Details of the design: 58

Magnetism: 58

Sound: 59

Microscopic examination: 59

Chapter 3: Prevention Techniques To Avoid Scams 61

Book 4: Protecting Your Coin Collection 65

Chapter 1: Best Practices For Collecting Coins 66

Chapter 2: Proper Handling And Storage Techniques 67

Chapter 3: Caring For And Cleaning Your Coins 70

Coin Cleaning: 71

Coin Storage 71

Chapter 4: Common Causes Of Damage To Coins 73

Environmental damage: 73

Mishandling: 74

Improper storage: 74

Chemical damage: 75

Chapter 5: Understanding Mint Coins 77

Book 5: Monetizing Your Coin Collection 78

Chapter 1: Essential Considerations Before Investing In Coins 79

Research: 79

Industry publications: 79

Auction houses: 80

Coin dealers: 80

Online marketplaces: 80

Numismatic associations: 80

Historical data: 80

Quality: 81

Rarity: 81

Liquidity: 81

Budget: 81

Storage: 81

Chapter 2: Strategies For Selling Coins 82

Timing: 82

Selling platform: 82

Grading and authentication: 82

Pricing: 83

Marketing: 83

Consignment: 83

Chapter 3: Top Websites For Coin Enthusiasts And Collectors 83

PCGS Website: 84

NGC Website: 84

Coin World Website: 84

American Numismatic Association Website: 84

Heritage Auctions Website: 85

Stack's Bowers Galleries Website:..85

The Red Book Website: 85

Chapter 4: Timing The Market For Maximum Profits 86

Research market trends: 86

Monitor supply and demand: 86

Seasonal trends:..87

Keep an eye on economic indicators:..87

Work with an auction company or trusted dealer: 87

Chapter 5: Price Guides And Pricing Tips 88

The Red Book.. 88

The Blue Book 89

Coin World Coin Values 89

NGC Price Guide 90

PCGS Price Guide 90

Heritage Auctions Price Guide 91

Pricing Tips For Buying And Selling Coins:...91

Chapter 6: The Coin Market Cycle 93

Introduction Stage: 93

Growth Stage: 93

Maturity Stage: 93

Decline Stage: 94

Bottoming Out Stage: 94

Recovery Stage: 94

Chapter 7: Navigating The Coin Dealing Industry 95

Chapter 8: Finding A Trusted Local Coin Dealer 97

Chapter 9: Mistakes To Avoid When Buying And Selling Coins 99

Failing to do your research: 99

Overpaying or underselling: 99

Failing to authenticate coins: 99

Not paying attention to grading: 100

Selling too quickly: 100

Failing to protect your coins: 100

Book 6: Discovering Rare Coins 101

Chapter 1: Locating Rare And Valuable Coins 102

Chapter 2: America's Rarest Coins 104

1933 Double Eagle 104

1913 Liberty Head Nickel 105

1894-S Barber Dime 105

1804 Silver Dollar 105

1915-S Panama-Pacific Exposition $50 Gold 106

Chapter 3: Rare Coins From Around The World 107

1344 Edward III Gold "Double Leopard" Florin (England) 107

1992 Gold 2000 Yuan (China) 108

1621 100 Ducats (Polish-Lithuanian Commonwealth) 108

2007 Queen Elizabeth II Million Dollar Coin (Canada) (Tie) 108

1899 Single 9 Pond (South Africa) (Tie) 109

723 Umayyad Gold Dinar (Islamic Umayyad Kingdom) 109

2007 1 Million Canadian Gold Maple Leaf 110

1368-1382 Venice, Italy Silver Grosso PCGS AU 110

Chapter 4: Best Practices For Buying And Selling Rare Coins 112

Book 7: The History Of Coin Collecting 113

Chapter 1: Tracing The Evolution Of Coin Collecting 114

Chapter 2: Current Practices: 116

Chapter 3: How Coin Collecting Has Shaped World History 118

Book 8: The Future Of Coin Collecting 120

Chapter 1: A Glimpse Into The Future Of Coin Collecting 121

Digital coins: 121

The growing interest in international coins: 122

Greater use of technology in coin grading: 122

Chapter 2: The Impact Of Technology On The Hobby 123

Online marketplaces: 123

Mobile apps: 123

Online databases: 123

Digital images: 124

Counterfeiting: 124

Chapter 3: The Role Of Coin Collecting In Preserving History 125

Numismatic research: 125

Archival value: 125

Conservation: 125

Education: 126

Book 9: Coin Collecting Around the World 127

Chapter 1: Asian Coinage: Symbols of Dynasties and Civilizations 128

Ancient Chinese Coins: 128

Coins of the Indian Subcontinent: 129

Japanese and Korean Coins: 129

Chapter 2: African Coinage: A Glimpse of Tribal Heritage and Colonial Impact 130

Ancient and Medieval African Coins: 130

Tribal Coins and Trade Beads: 130

Colonial Impact and Modern African Coinage: 131

Chapter 3: Oceanic and Island Nations: A Fusion of Culture and History . 132

Ancient and Traditional Currencies: 132

Colonial Legacies and Modern Coinage: 132

Pacific Island Nations: A Mosaic of Cultures: 133

Book 10: Step-by-Step Guide to Getting Rich with Coin Collecting 134

Chapter 1: Building a Profitable Foundation 135

The Potential Returns and the Art of Coin Investment 135

Collecting for Passion vs. Profit 135

Research Essentials 136

Setting Clear Financial Goals and Diversification 137

Chapter 2: Acquisition, Protection, and Growth 138

Identifying and Acquiring Key, Rare, and Historically Significant Coins 138

Negotiation Strategies and Building Relationships for Better Acquisitions 138

Advanced Storage, Security Measures, and Insuring Your Collection 139

Growing the Value of Your Collection through Community Engagement, Exhibitions, and Networking 139

Chapter 3: Maximizing Returns and Navigating Challenges 140

The Art of Selling: Timing the Market and Leveraging Various Sales Platforms 140

Tax Implications, Financial Management, and Understanding Market Downturns 140

Recognizing and Avoiding Pitfalls that Impact Profitability 141

Strategic Planning for Long-term Wealth Generation and Leaving a Legacy 141

Conclusion 142

Introduction

Coins are a tangible link to the past, allowing collectors to hold and examine artifacts that have survived for centuries or even millennia. And coin collectors are the ones who keep that link with the past and present intact and preserved. If you are someone who would love to engage in the coin-collecting hobby, then there is a lot more about coins that you need to learn at first. There is a whole science of searching, collecting, cleaning, and storing rare coins, and you are about to learn everything about it.

The Coin Collection Bible is an all-in-one resource designed to introduce new collectors to the basics of coin collecting. It is essential for anyone who is interested in starting a coin collection but doesn't know where to begin. This bible typically covers a range of topics, including the history and characteristics of coins, grading and valuation, buying and selling coins, and organizing a collection. It also provides guidance on how to identify and authenticate coins, as well as tips for building a collection. A good coin collection for beginners book will also include high-quality images of coins, as well as detailed descriptions and background information about each coin. This can help beginners to familiarize themselves with the various types of coins and become more confident in their ability to identify and evaluate coins. In addition to these core features, this guidebook also provides additional resources such as glossaries of terms, collector forums, and market analysis. These resources can help beginners to stay up-to-date with current trends and values in the coin-collecting world. Overall, a coin collection for beginners book is an excellent starting point for anyone who is interested in starting a coin collection. It can provide valuable information and guidance, as well as help beginners make informed decisions about their collections.

Book 1:
The Basics Of Coin Collecting

From ancient coins to modern ones, the study of coins can offer a glimpse into the history, culture, and art of different societies. Whether you're a beginner or an experienced collector, the world of numismatics can provide endless opportunities for discovery and learning. In this chapter, we will explore the basics of coin collecting, including the history of coins, the different types of coins, and the essentials of building a coin collection. Whether you're interested in collecting coins for their historical significance, their aesthetic appeal, or their monetary value, this chapter will provide you with the knowledge and tools to get started.

Chapter 1: What Is Coin Collecting?

In simple words, it is a hobby or practice of collecting and studying coins, paper currency, tokens, and other related objects. Coin collectors seek out and acquire coins for their historical, cultural, aesthetic, and monetary value. Some coin collectors specialize in specific types of coins, such as ancient coins, commemorative coins, or rare coins, while others may collect coins from a particular country or time period. Coin collectors may also study the history and manufacturing processes behind the coins they collect and may be interested in the artwork and design elements of the coins. Coin collecting can be a fascinating and rewarding hobby, as it allows collectors to appreciate the unique beauty and history of different coins, as well as to learn about the cultures and events that are represented by the coins.

Chapter 2: Who Collects Coins?

The allure of collecting coins lies not only in the historical and cultural significance of the coins themselves but also in the thrill of the hunt and the satisfaction of building a valuable and unique collection. But who are the people behind this fascinating hobby? Who collects coins, and what motivates them to do so? In this chapter, we will explore the diverse community of coin collectors, their backgrounds, their interests, and their reasons for pursuing this timeless pastime. Some common types of people who collect coins include:

History buffs

History buffs are a group of collectors who are particularly interested in the historical significance of coins. They collect coins from different time periods and countries to learn more about the past and often focus on specific themes or historical events. For example, a history buff who is interested in ancient civilizations may collect coins from ancient Greece or Rome, while someone who is interested in American history may collect coins from the colonial era or the Civil War. These collectors often research the historical context behind the coins they collect and may attend lectures or read books on numismatics to deepen their understanding. In addition to the historical significance of the coins, history buffs may also appreciate the artistic and design elements of the coins, as they often reflect the style and culture of the time in which they were first released.

Investors

Investors collecting coins is a common practice in the numismatic or coin-collecting world. Coin collecting can be a hobby or an investment, and many collectors and investors seek out rare and valuable coins to add to their collections or portfolios. Coins can be collected for their historical significance, artistic value, rarity, or as a store of value. Some investors collect coins as a hedge against inflation or economic uncertainty, while others collect for the potential appreciation in value over time. When investing in coins, it's important to do your research and educate yourself on the market and the specific coins you're interested in. Factors that can affect the value of coins include rarity, condition, historical significance, and market demand. There are many resources available to help coin collectors and investors, including coin shows, auction houses, and online marketplaces.

Art enthusiasts

Art enthusiasts may collect coins as part of their broader interest in artistic expression and aesthetics. Coins can be appreciated not only for their historical and monetary value but also for their artistic and design qualities. Many coins feature intricate designs, detailed engravings, and beautiful compositions that reflect the cultural and artistic styles of the time period in which they were created. For art enthusiasts, collecting coins can be a way to explore and appreciate the artistic expressions of different cultures and historical periods.

In addition to their aesthetic appeal, coins can also provide a unique and tangible connection to history. Coins often feature images of historical figures or significant events and can provide insight into the politics, culture, and economy of a particular time and place. Collecting coins can be a rewarding and educational pursuit for art enthusiasts, allowing them to appreciate and learn about the artistic and historical significance of different coins and cultures. As with any form of collecting, it's important to do research and work with reputable dealers and sellers to ensure that the coins you acquire are authentic and valuable.

Hobbyists

For hobbyists, coin collecting can be a fun and engaging pursuit that allows them to learn about different cultures, historical events, and monetary systems. Coins can be acquired through a variety of channels, such as coin shows, online marketplaces, or local coin shops. Hobbyists may choose to specialize in a particular type of coin, such as ancient coins, commemorative coins, or coins from a particular country or time period. They may also collect coins for their aesthetic qualities, such as the beauty of their design or the quality of their engraving. Coin collecting can also be a social activity, with hobbyists participating in coin clubs or attending coin shows and events to meet other collectors and learn more about the hobby. While hobbyist collectors may not necessarily be focused on the monetary value of their coins, there is still potential for appreciation in value over time.

Inheritors

Inheritors who receive coin collections as part of an estate may choose to continue the collection as a way of preserving the legacy of the original collector. They may also be interested in continuing the collection for their own personal interest and enjoyment or as a potential investment. Inheritors may need to take steps to properly care for and manage the coin collection they inherit. This may include organizing and cataloging the collection, ensuring proper storage and preservation, and seeking out professional appraisals or valuations to understand the value of the coins.

In some cases, inheritors may choose to sell all or part of the collection in order to liquidate assets or to distribute the proceeds among multiple beneficiaries. In this case, it is important to work with a reputable dealer or auction house to ensure a fair and accurate valuation of the coins and to ensure a smooth transaction. Regardless of whether they choose to keep or sell the coin collection, inheritors may also need to consider tax implications associated with inheriting and/or selling the coins. It may be helpful to consult with a financial advisor or tax professional to understand these considerations and make informed decisions.

Chapter 3:
The Benefits And Joys Of Coin Collecting

Coin collecting, also known as numismatics, is a popular hobby enjoyed by millions of people around the world. For some, it is a means of preserving history, while for others, it is a way of investing and generating income. Regardless of the motivation, coin collecting offers a variety of benefits and joys that can be experienced by anyone who has a passion for it. From the thrill of discovering a rare coin to the satisfaction of completing a collection, this chapter explores the many ways in which coin collecting can enrich your life and provide endless hours of entertainment and fulfillment. Whether you are a seasoned collector or just starting out, there is something for everyone in the exciting world of numismatics.

Learning about history and culture

Coins offer a unique window into the past, as they often depict images of historical figures, events, and cultural symbols. Coin collecting is a great way to learn about history and culture, as coins offer a unique window into the past. Coins can reveal important information about the politics, economy, and cultural values of the time period in which they were created. For example, ancient coins can offer insight into the art, mythology, and political systems of ancient civilizations such as Greece and Rome. Coins from the Middle Ages can reveal information about the feudal system, while coins from the Renaissance can provide a glimpse into the artistic and cultural achievements of that time period.

Coins can also be used to study the economic and social history of a particular region or country. The design, composition, and metal content of coins can reveal information about the availability and value of natural resources, as well as the monetary policies and economic systems of a particular time and place. Collectors who are interested in learning about history and culture through coin collecting can also benefit from studying the historical context of the coins they collect. This may include reading books or articles about the history of the time period or region in which the coins were minted, as well as consulting with experts in the field.

Appreciating the artistry of coins:

Coin collecting is also a great way to appreciate the artistry of coins. Coins can be viewed as miniature works of art that reflect the culture, style, and craftsmanship of the time period in which they were created. Coins can feature intricate engravings, detailed portraits, and depictions of mythological figures, animals, or important events. The designs can reflect the artistic styles of the time period, as well as the cultural values and beliefs of the people who created them.

Collectors can appreciate the artistry of coins by studying the details and composition of the design. They can also compare different coins from the same or different time periods to observe the evolution of the design and the changing artistic styles. Coins can be made from various metals. The different materials and finishes can be used to create interesting textures, contrast, and depth in the design. In addition to the design of the coin itself, collectors can also appreciate the historical context and significance of the coin. For example, a coin that was minted to commemorate an important historical event may have a design that reflects that event, adding to the cultural and historical value of the coin.

Social interaction:

Coin collecting can be a social activity, with hobbyists participating in coin clubs or attending coin shows and events to meet other collectors and learn more about the hobby. Joining a coin club is a great way to meet other collectors who share your passion for coins. You can attend meetings, events, and shows where you can interact with other collectors and learn more about the hobby.

Coin shows are a great way to interact with other collectors, dealers, and experts in the field. You can attend seminars and workshops, buy, sell, or trade coins, and connect with others who share your interest in coins. There are many online forums and discussion boards where you can connect with other collectors and enthusiasts. You can share your collection, ask for advice, and engage in discussions about the history, value, and authenticity of coins. You can organize coin swaps or exchanges with other collectors to expand your collection and interact with others who share your interest in coins. This can be a fun and engaging way to build your collection and connect with other collectors. Attending auctions or estate sales can be a great way to connect with other collectors and acquire valuable coins. You can interact with other bidders and learn more about the history and value of the coins being auctioned. While not the primary reason for collecting, there is potential for the value of coins to appreciate over time. Collectors may be able to build a valuable collection that can be passed down as a family heirloom or sold for a profit. Coin collecting can potentially be a valuable investment opportunity, as certain coins can appreciate in value over time. Here are some factors to consider when building a coin collection for potential appreciation in value:

Historical significance:

Coins that have historical significance or are associated with important events, individuals, or periods can be highly sought after by collectors. These coins may increase in value as their historical significance becomes more widely recognized.

Condition: The condition of a coin can greatly impact its value. Coins that are in excellent condition and have not been damaged or cleaned are generally more valuable than those that have been heavily circulated or have significant wear and tear.

Market demand: The demand for certain types of coins can fluctuate over time. As collectors' interests and preferences change, the value of certain coins may increase or decrease. Understanding market trends and demand can help you make informed decisions when building your collection.

Expertise and research: Researching and understanding the coins you collect is important when building a collection for potential appreciation in value. Seek out expert advice and reliable resources to help you identify valuable coins, understand their history and rarity, and make informed purchasing decisions.

It's important to note that, like any investment, there is risk involved in coin collecting, and there is no guarantee that a coin collection will appreciate in value. However, building a diverse and well-researched collection can increase the chances of potential appreciation in value over time.

Challenge and excitement:

Collecting coins can be a challenging and exciting pursuit, as collectors work to acquire rare or hard-to-find coins and complete sets. Coin collecting can be a challenging and exciting hobby that provides a sense of achievement and satisfaction. Searching for rare and valuable coins can be an exciting challenge that requires time, effort, and knowledge. This can involve attending auctions, estate sales, coin shows, and online marketplaces to search for unique and rare coins. Building a complete set of coins can be a fun and rewarding challenge that requires patience and persistence. This can involve collecting a series of coins from a specific time period, country, or theme. Coin collecting involves learning about the history and artistry of coins. This can be a fascinating and challenging pursuit that requires research, analysis, and appreciation for the beauty and craftsmanship of different coins. Coin collecting can offer a sense of excitement and discovery as collectors come across new and unexpected coins. This can involve exploring new sources for coins and identifying unique or unusual pieces for their collection. Interacting with other collectors and sharing knowledge and information can provide a sense of excitement and challenge as collectors learn from each other and discover new aspects of the hobby. Overall, coin collecting can be a fulfilling and enjoyable hobby with many benefits and joys. Whether you're interested in history, art, or simply building a collection, coin collecting can offer a unique and rewarding experience.

Chapter 4: Types Of Coins To Collect

One of the greatest aspects of coin collecting is the variety of coins available for collectors to pursue. From ancient coins to modern-day currency, there are countless types of coins to choose from, each with its unique history, design, and value. Deciding which coins to collect can be a daunting task, especially for beginners, but it is a critical step in building a meaningful and fulfilling collection. This chapter will explore the different types of coins that collectors can pursue, including rare coins, commemorative coins, bullion coins, and many others. We'll dive into the unique characteristics of each type of coin, their respective histories and significance, and the factors that impact their value. Whether you're a seasoned collector or a beginner, this chapter will help you understand the various options available and guide you toward choosing the right coins for your collection.

Historical coins:

Historical coins are a popular type of coin collecting that involves assembling a collection of coins that have historical significance or are associated with important events, individuals, or periods. Historical coins can offer a fascinating window into the past, providing a tangible link to the people, places, and cultures of earlier times. Here are some examples of historical coins that collectors may consider: Ancient coins can be some of the oldest and most historically significant coins that collectors can acquire. These coins can come from civilizations such as Greece, Rome, Persia, and China and can provide a glimpse into the cultures and economies of the ancient world. Colonial coins were produced by early European colonizers in the New World. These coins can include Spanish "cob" coins, British "cartwheel" pennies, and French "jetons," among others.

Collectors may choose to focus on coins from a particular country or empire, such as the United States, England, France, or Rome, for example. These coins can provide insight into the economic and political history of a particular place and time. Collecting historical coins can be a fascinating and educational pursuit, providing collectors with an opportunity to connect with the past and gain a deeper appreciation for the people and events that have shaped the world. However, due to their rarity and historical significance, historical coins can be expensive and difficult to obtain, making them a more challenging and rewarding aspect of coin collecting.

Rare coins:

Rare coins are a popular type of coin collecting that involves acquiring coins that are rare, unique, or otherwise difficult to obtain. Rare coins can be highly sought after by collectors due to their historical significance, cultural or artistic value, or their scarcity. Here are some examples of rare coins that collectors may consider:

Error coins:

Error coins are coins that have been produced with some kind of mistake or error, either in the minting process or in the design. These mistakes can range from minor imperfections to major errors that render the coin highly valuable to collectors. Some common types of error coins include:

Doubled dies: This occurs when a design is imprinted onto a coin more than once, resulting in a slightly blurred or doubled image.

Off-center strikes: This happens when a coin is struck off-center, resulting in an uneven design.

Clipped planchets: This happens when a blank metal disk used for striking a coin is cut incompletely, resulting in a missing portion of the coin.

Broad strikes: This happens when a coin is struck outside the collar used to hold the blank metal disk in place, resulting in a coin without a rim.

Die cracks: This occurs when the dies used to strike the coin develop a crack, causing an imperfect design on the coin.

Repunched mint marks: This happens when the mint mark is punched onto the die more than once, resulting in a slightly offset mint mark.

Error coins are generally rare and can be highly valuable to collectors, depending on the rarity and the nature of the error. Collectors often seek out error coins as they add a unique element to their collections.

Proof coins:

Proof coins are special coins that are struck using specially prepared dies, planchets, and highly polished blanks. These coins are made using a more precise minting process, resulting in a coin with a highly reflective surface, sharp details, and a frosted design that appears to float above the mirrored background. Proof coins are often made in limited quantities and are not intended for circulation, making them highly collectible. They are typically sold directly by the mint or by authorized dealers, and they often come in protective cases and with a certificate of authenticity. The history of proof coins dates back to the 17th century, when they were originally produced to ensure the accuracy and quality of the minting process. Today, proof coins are produced for collectors and investors, and they are often made in precious metals (like silver and gold).

The design of proof coins can vary from standard designs to commemorative designs, and they can feature a variety of themes, such as historical events, famous people, and cultural icons. Proof coins are highly sought after by collectors, and they can command high prices in the collector's market.

Commemorative coins: Commemorative coins are coins that were minted to commemorate a particular event or individual. These coins can be rare due to their limited production and historical significance.

Coins with historical or cultural significance: Coins that are associated with important historical figures, events, or cultures can be highly valuable and rare. For example, coins from ancient Greece or Rome can be rare and valuable due to their historical significance and cultural value.

Collecting rare coins can be a challenging and rewarding pursuit, providing collectors with an opportunity to acquire unique and valuable pieces of history. However, due to their rarity, rare coins can be expensive and difficult to obtain, making them a more advanced and specialized aspect of coin collecting.

Bullion coins:

Bullion coins are a type of coin that is made primarily from precious metal, such as gold, silver, platinum, or palladium, and are typically bought and sold based on the value of the metal it contains. Bullion coins are often produced by government mints, and their purity and weight are guaranteed by the issuing authority. One of the main reasons that people invest in bullion coins is to hedge against inflation and protect their wealth. The value of precious metals tends to rise in times of economic uncertainty, and holding bullion coins can provide a safe haven for investors seeking to diversify their portfolios. Bullion coins come in a variety of sizes, ranging from small fractional coins to larger, full-ounce coins.

In addition to their investment value, bullion coins can also have collectible value, particularly for rare or limited edition coins. It's important to note that the value of bullion coins can be volatile and is subject to fluctuations in the global precious metals market. Investors in bullion coins should carefully consider their investment goals and seek the advice of professionals before making any purchases.

Commemorative coins:

Commemorative coins are coins that are issued to honor a particular person, event, or organization. These coins are often minted in limited quantities and can be made of various precious metals (like platinum, silver, and gold). Commemorative coins can be issued by governments, central banks, or private organizations. They are often used to mark important historical or cultural events, such as the Olympic Games, royal weddings, or significant anniversaries. In addition to their face value as legal tender, commemorative coins often have additional value due to their rarity and the significance of the event or person they commemorate. Collectors may be willing to pay a premium for these coins, especially if they are in excellent condition or come with special packaging or certificates of authenticity. It's important to note that commemorative coins are different from circulating coins, which are issued for everyday use as legal tender. While commemorative coins may have a nominal face value, their primary value comes from their collectability and historical significance.

Foreign coins:

Collecting coins from different countries can offer a unique and diverse collection that reflects different cultures, histories, and aesthetics. Foreign coins are coins that are issued by a country other than the one in which they are currently being used. They can be acquired through a variety of means, such as traveling abroad, receiving them as gifts, or purchasing them from coin dealers or online marketplaces. Foreign coins can be valuable to collectors for a number of reasons, including their rarity, historical significance, and aesthetic appeal.

In addition to their collectible value, foreign coins can also have a practical use for travelers or individuals who do business with other countries. Some foreign coins may be readily exchangeable at banks or currency exchange kiosks, while others may need to be exchanged through specialty dealers. It is important to note that the value of foreign coins can vary greatly depending on factors such as their condition, rarity, and market demand. Collectors and investors should do their research and seek the advice of professionals before buying or selling foreign coins.

Coin sets:

Collecting a complete set of coins can be a challenging and rewarding pursuit. This can include collecting a series of coins from a specific time period, country, or theme. Coin sets are a popular type of coin collecting that involves assembling a complete set of coins from a specific time period, country, or theme. Coin sets can include a series of coins that were issued by a government, such as a complete set of U.S. quarters or a set of Australian lunar coins, or a series of coins that were designed to commemorate a particular event or individual. Here are some popular types of coin sets that collectors may consider:

- Proof sets: Proof sets are collections of coins that have been specially minted for collectors. These coins have a high level of detail and a mirror-like finish and are often sold in sets that include multiple denominations of coins.
- Mint sets: Mint sets are collections of coins that were produced by a particular mint during a particular year. These sets can include coins that were produced for circulation as well as coins that were produced for collectors.
- Commemorative sets: Commemorative sets are collections of coins that were issued to commemorate a particular event or individual. These sets can include coins with special designs or features and are often produced in limited quantities.
- Type sets: Type sets are collections of coins that represent a particular type of coin from a given time period or country. For example, a U.S.-type set might include one coin from each denomination that was produced by the U.S. Mint from a particular time period.
- Year sets: Year sets are collections of coins that were issued by a particular country or mint during a particular year. These sets can include coins that were produced for circulation as well as coins that were produced for collectors.

Ultimately, the types of coins that collectors may choose to collect depending on their personal interests and goals. Collectors can choose to focus on a particular type of coin or create a diverse collection that reflects a variety of interests and aesthetics.

Chapter 5: Essential Numismatic Terms

The world of numismatics has a rich vocabulary of terms and jargon that can be challenging to navigate, especially for those who are new to coin collecting. Understanding the language of numismatics is essential for effective communication among collectors, dealers, and other industry professionals, and it is critical for making informed decisions about coins. This chapter will provide an overview of some of the essential numismatic terms that collectors should be familiar with, from basic coin grading terminology to more advanced concepts such as die varieties and mint marks. Whether you're a beginner or an experienced collector looking to expand your knowledge, this chapter will help you build a solid foundation of numismatic terminology and increase your confidence in the world of coin collecting.

Alloy:

It is a homogeneous mixture of at least two metals, sometimes more than two metals, or a mixture of metal with a non-metal. Alloys are created by melting two or more metals together and then allowing them to cool and solidify, resulting in a new material that has properties that are different from the original metals. The properties of an alloy depend on the specific metals that are used, as well as the proportions in which they are combined.

American Numismatic Association (ANA):

It is an organization (non-profit) created to promote the research and collection of coins, paper currency, tokens, and medals. Founded in 1891, the ANA has over 25,000 members in the United States and around the globe. The ANA offers a wide range of resources and services to its members, including educational programs, a library and research center, a museum, a monthly magazine, and a network of local clubs and specialty groups. The organization also holds an annual convention, which is the largest gathering of coin collectors in the world.

Annealing:

Annealing is a heat treatment process used to modify the properties of a material, typically a metal or an alloy. The process involves heating the material to a specific temperature and then cooling it slowly, often in a controlled atmosphere. Annealing is used to reduce hardness, improve ductility, and increase toughness.

Assay:

An assay is a chemical analysis that is used to determine the composition or purity of a substance. The term "assay" is commonly used in the context of testing the quality of metals and minerals, but it can also refer to the analysis of pharmaceuticals, foods, and other substances.

Bag Mark:

A bag mark is a small scratch or dents on the top of a coin, typically occurring by contact with other coins in a bag during transport or storage. Bag marks can occur on both uncirculated and circulated coins, and they can affect the coin's overall appearance and value.

Bi-Metallic:

Bi-metallic refers to a coin or other object that is made from two different types of metal. Typically, a bi-metallic coin has a core made of one type of metal and an outer ring or border made of another type of metal. The two metals are bonded together using a special process, such as milling or striking.

Blank:

The term "blank" in numismatics refers to a piece of metal that has been cut or stamped into a blank disk or planchet that will be used to make a coin. Blanks are typically made from strips of metal that are rolled and then cut into circular pieces of a specific size and weight.

Bullion:

Bullion refers to a type of precious metal, such as gold, silver, or platinum, that is valued primarily for its intrinsic metal content rather than for its face value as currency. Bullion can take the form of bars, ingots, or coins, and it is typically produced by private mints or government mints around the world.

Business Strike:

The term "business strike" is a numismatic term that refers to a coin that is struck for circulation and intended for general use as currency. Business strikes are typically produced in large quantities and may be made of a variety of metals, depending on the country and the time period in which the coins were produced.

Bust:

In numismatics, the term "bust" refers to a design element found on many coins and medals, typically located on the obverse (front) side of the coin. A bust is a portrait or depiction of a person's head, shoulders, and upper chest and is usually shown in profile or facing forward.

Clad Coinage:

Clad coinage refers to coins that are made of two or more layers of different metals. The term "clad" is derived from the Latin word "claudere," meaning "to close" or "to encase," and refers to the way in which the layers of metal are bonded together to create the coin. Clad coinage was first introduced in the United States in the 1960s as a way to reduce the cost of producing coins. Prior to this, most coins were made of a single metal, such as gold, silver, or copper, which had a higher intrinsic value and was, therefore, more expensive to produce.

Collar:

In numismatics, a collar is a device used in the minting process to help control the size and shape of a coin. The collar is a circular ring or sleeve that is placed around the blank piece of metal, called a planchet, before it is struck by the coin die.

Condition:

"Condition" is a numismatic term that refers to the state of preservation or quality of a coin. It is an important factor that determines the value of a coin. Coins that are in better condition are generally more valuable than those in poor condition.

Counterfeit:

In numismatics, counterfeit refers to a fake or imitation coin or banknote that is made to deceive collectors, investors, or the general public. Counterfeit coins or banknotes may be made with the intention of passing them off as genuine in order to make a profit or to deceive someone.

Currency:

In numismatics, the term "currency" is used to refer to any type of money that is used as a medium of exchange, such as banknotes or coins. Currency can be issued by governments, central banks, or other monetary authorities. In the context of coin collecting, the term "currency" may specifically refer to coins that were intended for use as money, as opposed to commemorative or Medallic issues. Currency coins typically have a design and composition that is optimized for use in commerce, with features such as high durability, standard weight and size, and distinctive designs that make them easy to identify and authenticate.

Denomination:

In numismatics, the term "denomination" refers to the face value or monetary value given to a particular coin, banknote, etc. Denominations are typically expressed in a specific currency unit, such as dollars, euros, or pounds, and may vary widely depending on the time period, country, and issuing authority.

Die:

The term "die" is a numismatic term that refers to the metal piece used to strike a coin or medal. It is a cylindrical piece of metal that has an incuse (negative) image of the design of the coin or medal on one end. When the die is struck against a blank piece of metal, it leaves an impression of the design on the metal.

Edge:

The edge of a coin is another important numismatic term that refers to the outermost perimeter of the coin. The edge is part of the coin that runs around its circumference and is usually raised or reeded, providing a texture and visual distinction from the flat surfaces of the obverse and reverse.

Engraver:

In the context of numismatics, engravers are responsible for creating the images and inscriptions that appear on coins, medals, and other metal objects. They work closely with mint officials and other stakeholders to ensure that the designs they create are both aesthetically pleasing and historically accurate.

Error:

In numismatics, an error is a mistake or deviation from the standard production process that results in a coin or medal that is different from what was intended. Errors can occur at various stages of the minting process, including design, blank preparation, striking, and finishing.

Face Value:

In numismatics, the face value is the nominal or stated value of a coin or other monetary item. It is the value that is inscribed on the coin by the issuing authority and is typically expressed in the currency of the issuing country. For example, the face value of a United States dime is 10 cents, while the face value of a British pound coin is 1 pound.

Field:
In numismatics, the term "field" refers to the flat, unraised part of a coin's top surface that is not occupied by an inscription, design, or other elements. The field is typically smooth and serves as a background against which the design of the coin stands out.

Grade:
In numismatics, grade refers to the condition of a coin or medal, as assessed by a trained grader or expert. The grade of a coin is an important factor in determining its value and collectability, as higher-grade coins are generally more desirable and rare than lower-grade coins.

Hairlines:
In numismatics, the term "hairlines" refers to very fine, shallow scratches or lines that are visible on the top surface of a coin. Hairlines happen due to a variety of factors, including improper handling, cleaning, or storage, and can detract from the overall appearance and grade of a coin.

Incuse:
In numismatics, the term "incuse" refers to a type of design or inscription that is impressed into the surface of a coin rather than raised above it. Incuse designs are created by striking the coin from a die with a recessed design, which leaves a depressed, or incuse, image on the coin's surface.

Ingot:
In numismatics, an ingot is a type of bar or brick made of precious metal, such as gold or silver. Ingots are typically made through a process of melting and casting the metal into a specific shape and are often used as a store of value or for investment purposes.

Inscription:
An inscription refers to any text that appears on a coin or medal. Inscriptions can include a variety of information, such as the name of the issuing authority, the denomination or value of the coin, the date of minting, and other information.

Intrinsic Value (Bullion Value):
Intrinsic value, also known as bullion value, refers to the value of a coin or medal based on the worth of the metal it contains. The intrinsic value of a coin is identified by its weight and fineness, or purity, of the metal and is calculated based on the current market price of the metal.

Key Date:
In numismatics, the term "key date" refers to a coin that is considered to be particularly rare or valuable due to its low mintage or other unique characteristics. Key dates are typically the most sought-after coins in a particular series or denomination and are often the cornerstone of a coin collection.

Legal Tender:
In numismatics, legal tender refers to a coin or banknote that is recognized as an official medium of exchange by a government. A legal tender is a form of currency that is accepted as payment for debts and taxes and must be accepted by merchants and other businesses as a means of payment.

Legend:
In numismatics, a legend refers to the lettering or inscription on a coin or medal that includes important identifying information. The legend often includes the name of the ruler or issuing authority, the date, and the denomination or value of the coin.

Medal:
In numismatics, a medal is a metallic object that is similar in appearance to a coin but is not intended to serve as a form of currency. Medals are typically awarded to individuals

or groups as a form of recognition for a specific achievement or contribution and often feature intricate designs and inscriptions.

Medium of Exchange:
A medium of exchange refers to any form of currency or payment that is accepted by a society or group of people as a means of exchanging goods and services. This can include physical objects such as coins and banknotes, as well as other forms of payment such as digital currency or bartering.

Mint Luster:
Mint luster is a term used in numismatics to describe the reflective quality of a newly-minted coin's surface. When a coin is struck by a mint, the metal is compressed, causing it to flatten and become smoother. This process can create a reflective surface on the coin, which is known as mint luster.

Mint Mark:
It is a small emblem or letter found on a coin that indicates which mint facility produced the coin. They can be important for collectors and historians, as they can help identify where and when a particular coin was produced.

Mint State:
It is the condition of a coin that has never been circulated and retains its original mint luster. Coins in mint state are considered to be in excellent condition and are highly valued by collectors.

Motto:
A motto is a brief phrase or sentence that is inscribed on a coin. Mottos can convey a variety of messages, from political slogans to religious sentiments, and are often used to add meaning or symbolism to a coin's design.

Mylar:

Mylar is a type of polyester film that is commonly used in numismatics for coin preservation and storage. Mylar is a durable, chemically stable material that is resistant to tearing, moisture, and other forms of damage, making it an ideal material for long-term coin storage.

Numismatics:

It is the study of coins, currencies, and related objects that have been used as a medium of exchange, a commemorative item, or an art form. The word "numismatics" comes from the Greek word "nomisma," meaning "coin."

Obsolete:

"Obsolete" refers to coins or currencies that are no longer in circulation and are considered no longer legal tender. These coins or currencies may have been replaced by a new design or series or may have been discontinued altogether.

Obverse:

The "obverse" of a coin refers to the front or head side of the coin, which typically features the main design elements, such as the portrait of a person, the emblem of a country or organization, or other decorative or symbolic elements.

Off-Center:

An "off-center" coin refers to a coin that was struck with the design elements positioned outside of the center of the planchet. This can occur during the minting process if the planchet is not properly aligned with the dies or if the dies themselves are misaligned.

Overstrike:

An "overstrike" occurs when a coin is struck over an existing coin or other objects. Overstriking was a common practice in ancient times when coins were often melted down and re-minted with a new design, but it can also occur accidentally during the minting process.

Pattern:

A "pattern" refers to a trial or experimental coin that is created as a prototype for a new design or series of coins. Patterns are often produced in small quantities and are not intended for circulation but are instead used for evaluation, testing, or display purposes.

Planchet:

A "planchet" refers to a blank piece of metal that is used to make a coin. Planchets are typically made from strips or sheets of metal that are cut to the correct size and shape for the desired denomination and design of the coin.

Proof Set:

A "proof set" is a collection of coins that have been specially produced using a minting process that results in a high-quality, mirror-like finish. Proof sets are typically sold to collectors and often include coins of different denominations or designs.

Relief:

"relief" refers to the height or depth of the design elements on a coin relative to the surface of the coin. A high-relief design has elements that are raised significantly above the surface of the coin, while a low-relief design has elements that are more shallow or flat.

Restrike:

A "restrike" refers to a coin that has been struck from a die that was created after the original production run of the coin. Restrikes are often made for commemorative purposes or to meet the demand for a particular coin that has become scarce or rare.

Reverse:

The "reverse" refers to the back side of a coin, as opposed to the "obverse," which is the front side. The other side of a coin typically features a different design or image on the obverse and may include additional information such as the denomination or issuing authority.

Riddler:

A "riddler" is a machine that is used to sort and grade coins based on their size and weight. The term "riddler" comes from the process of sifting or riddling through a large number of coins to separate out those that do not meet a certain size or weight standard.

Rim:

The "rim" refers to the raised edge around the coin. The rim serves several important functions, including protecting the design and legends from wear and damage, helping to prevent the coin from being shaved or clipped, and providing a surface to aid in stacking or counting coins.

Roll:

A "roll" refers to a number of coins that have been packaged together in a paper or plastic wrapper. Rolls are typically used to store and transport large quantities of coins and are commonly sold by banks, coin dealers, and other sellers.

Series:

The term "series" refers to a group of coins that share a common design or motif and are typically issued over a period of time. Series can be based on various factors, such as the issuing authority, the time period of issuance, or the specific design elements.

Slab:

A "slab" is a term used to refer to a plastic holder used to encapsulate and protect a coin. Slabs are typically made of hard, transparent plastic and are designed to provide a secure, tamper-evident container for individual coins.

Strike:

The term "strike" refers to the process of stamping a design onto a blank piece of metal to create a coin. The quality of the strike is an important factor in evaluating the quality and value of a coin.

Type Set:
A type set is a collection of coins that represents a specific set of coin types rather than a comprehensive collection of all coins produced by a particular mint or country. A type set might include one example of each major design or denomination produced by a particular mint or country.

Uncirculated:
"Uncirculated" refers to the condition of a coin that has never been used as currency and is in essentially the same condition as when it left the mint. Uncirculated coins have not been worn, scratched, or damaged in any way, and they retain their original mint luster.

Upsetting Mill:
An upsetting mill is a device used in the process of minting coins to raise the rim or edge of a blank coin disc, making it easier to produce a uniform and well-defined edge on the finished coin.

Variety:
A variety refers to a specific subtype or variation of a particular coin design. Coins can have a wide range of variations, such as differences in the placement of design elements, changes in the size or shape of certain features, or variations in the metal composition or minting process.

Book 2:
Evaluating Coin Value

Evaluating the value of a coin is an essential aspect of coin collecting, and it requires a combination of knowledge, experience, and research. Whether you are a beginner or a seasoned collector, the ability to accurately assess the value of a coin is critical for making informed buying and selling decisions. In this book, we will explore the various factors that determine a coin's value, from its rarity and historical significance to its condition and market demand. We will also discuss the different methods and tools used to evaluate coins, including coin grading, price guides, and auction records. By the end of this book, you will have a comprehensive understanding of how to evaluate the value of coins and make informed decisions in the world of numismatics.

Chapter 1:
How To Determine A Coin's Worth

Determining the worth of a coin is a crucial skill for any coin collector or investor. The value of a coin can be influenced by several factors, such as its rarity, condition, historical significance, and current market demand. It can be a challenging task to determine the worth of a coin accurately, especially for those who are new to coin collecting. However, with the right knowledge and tools, anyone can learn how to determine a coin's value. In this chapter, we will explore the various steps and methods used to assess a coin's worth. Here are some general steps that you can follow to get an idea of a coin's worth for collection:

Research:
Begin by researching the coin in question to learn more about its history and significance. Look for information on the year it was minted, the country of origin, and any notable events or figures that are featured on the coin. This will help you understand the coin's context and historical significance, which can affect its value.

Assess condition:
The condition is a key factor in knowing the value of a coin. Look for signs of wear, such as scratches, dents, or discoloration. The less damaged a coin is, the more value it is likely to have. In general, coins that have not been circulated (known as "uncirculated" coins) are more valuable than those that have been used.

Check rarity:
The rarity of a coin can also affect its value. Coins that were produced in limited quantities or that are no longer in circulation are likely to be more valuable than more

common coins. Look up the mintage figures for the certain coins you are interested in to get an idea of how rare it is.

Consider demand:

The demand for a particular coin can also impact its value. Some coins may be in high demand among collectors, driving up their value. Look for recent sales of similar coins to get an idea of the current market value.

Consult experts:

If you are unsure about the value of a coin, consider consulting with a professional coin appraiser or dealer. They can provide you with a more accurate assessment based on their expertise and knowledge of the current market. Keep in mind that the value of a coin can fluctuate over time based on factors such as market demand and conditions. It is important to stay informed and regularly reassess the value of your coin collection.

Chapter 2:
The Role Of Grading In Coin Value

Coin grading is an essential part of determining a coin's value. The physical condition is a significant factor in assessing a coin's worth, and grading provides a standardized and objective way of evaluating a coin's condition. Grading considers factors such as the wear and tear of the coin, its luster, and any blemishes or damage that may affect its appearance. The grading process assigns a numerical value on a scale from 1 to 70, with 1 being the lowest grade and 70 being the highest.

The grading process involves several steps. First, the coin is examined for any signs of wear, such as scratches, dents, or discoloration. Next, the coin's luster is evaluated to determine its shine and reflectivity. The coin's strike is also assessed to determine the quality of the design, including any details that may be missing or unclear. Finally, the overall appeal of the coin is considered, including any blemishes or damage that may affect its appearance. The grading scale used in the coin-collecting industry is the Sheldon grading scale, which was developed by Dr. William Sheldon in the 1940s. The scale ranges from 1 to 70, with 1 being the lowest grade and 70 being the highest. A coin graded as one is considered to be barely recognizable, while a coin graded as 70 is considered to be perfect and without any visible flaws.

The grade of a coin has a significant impact on its value. Coins with higher grades are generally more valuable than those with lower grades, as they are considered to be in better condition and more desirable to collectors. Additionally, the difference in value between two grades can be significant, with even a small change in grade resulting in a large change in value. It's important to note that grading is not an exact science and can be subject to some variation based on the grader's personal interpretation. Therefore, it's essential to choose a reputable grading service and to familiarize yourself with the grading scale and process to make informed decisions about your coin collection.

Chapter 3:
A Guide To Understanding Coin Values

Coins have been used as a form of currency for thousands of years and have evolved into a fascinating field of study known as numismatics. One of the key aspects of coin collecting is understanding the value of the coins in your collection. A coin's value is determined by a variety of factors. This chapter will serve as a guide to understanding coin values and the factors that influence them, providing an overview of key concepts and strategies for evaluating and valuing coins. Whether you are a seasoned collector or just starting out, this guide will help you navigate the complex world of coin values and make informed decisions about building and maintaining your collection. Here are some key factors that can affect a coin's value:

Rarity:

Coins that are rare or have a limited mintage are generally more valuable than those that are more common. Coins from certain years or with certain features may be particularly rare, which can drive up their value. The rarity of a coin is a key factor that can affect its value. Generally, the rarer a coin is, the more valuable it is to collectors. There are a few different factors that can contribute to a coin's rarity, including:

Mintage:

Mintage refers to the number of coins produced by a mint for a specific coin issue. It is an important factor that affects the rarity and value of a coin. The mintage of a coin can vary greatly depending on several factors, such as the denomination of the coin, the time period in which it was produced, and the purpose of the coin. For example, commemorative coins often have lower mintages because they are produced to mark a specific event or occasion, while regular circulation coins tend to have higher mintages to meet the demand for everyday use.

The mintage of coins can also be affected by production issues, such as errors or problems with the production process. Coins with lower-than-expected mintages due to production issues are often highly sought after by collectors, as they are rare and unique. It's important to note that the mintage of a coin does not always correlate with its value. Other factors, such as the condition of the coin, its rarity, and its historical significance, can all influence its value in the coin market.

Survival rate:

The survival rate of coins refers to the percentage of coins that have survived over time and still exist today. It is difficult to determine the exact survival rate of coins because it varies depending on the specific coin issue, time period, and the circumstances surrounding the coin's production, use, and preservation. In general, older coins tend to have lower survival rates because they have been in circulation for longer periods and may have been more susceptible to wear and tear damage or loss.

For example, ancient coins, such as those from the Roman or Greek era, often have very low survival rates due to the passage of time, the fact that they were made from softer metals like silver and gold that are easily worn down, and the fact that they were often used as currency and may have been melted down for their precious metal content. On the other hand, coins from the modern era may have higher survival rates due to improved production methods, better storage and preservation techniques, and the fact that many modern coins are collected and kept as numismatic items. The survival rate of a coin is an important factor in determining its rarity and value in the coin market. Coins with low survival rates, such as those from ancient civilizations or rare or highly collectible issues, tend to be more valuable and sought after by collectors.

Varieties and errors:

Varieties and errors in coin production can also make certain coins rare and valuable. For example, a coin that was accidentally struck with the wrong design or with a double strike may be more valuable to collectors. Varieties and errors are types of coins that are different from the standard version of a particular coin issue. These coins can be highly sought after by collectors because they are often rare, unique, and have interesting stories behind them. Varieties of coins can be caused by a variety of factors, such as different die types, mint marks, or other design features that distinguish them from the standard version of the coin. For example, a coin may have a different design on its other side, slightly different size or weight, or different wording or inscriptions than the standard version.

Errors, on the other hand, are coins that have been produced with mistakes or defects. These can include things like wrong or missing dates, doubled or tripled letters or numbers, off-center strikes, or other types of production errors. Some errors are the result of mistakes made during the production process, while others are the result of intentional actions taken by mint workers. Like varieties, errors can be highly prized by collectors. The more significant the error or variety, the rarer the coin and the more valuable it is likely to be.

Historical significance:

The historical significance of a coin can be an important factor in assessing its value. Coins that have played a significant role in history or that are associated with important events, figures, or periods are often highly prized by collectors and can command high prices in the coin market. The historical significance of a coin can come from a number of different sources. For example, a coin may have been produced to commemorate an important event, such as a war or the coronation of a monarch. It may have been used in trade or commerce in a particular region or period, or it may have been produced using unique or unusual methods or materials.

The historical context in which a coin was produced, circulated, or used can also be important in assessing its value. For example, a coin may have been produced during a particularly important or innovative period in history, or it may have been produced under unusual or rare circumstances, such as during a period of political or economic upheaval. The historical significance of a coin can also be influenced by its provenance or ownership history. Coins that have been owned by important figures or have been part of famous collections can be particularly valuable.

Determining the rarity of a coin can be challenging, as it often requires research and knowledge of the particular coin and its history. Resources such as price guides and online marketplaces can be helpful in identifying rare coins and determining their value. It's important to be cautious when purchasing rare coins, as there are many counterfeit coins on the market. Working with reputable dealers and using third-party authentication services can help ensure that you are purchasing genuine coins.

Condition:

Coins that are in better condition are generally more valuable than coins that are in poor condition or have been heavily worn or damaged. The condition of a coin is typically assessed using a grading system that evaluates the coin's appearance and level of wear. The most widely used grading system is the Sheldon Scale, which assigns a numerical grade to a coin based on its level of wear and the amount of detail that remains visible on the coin.

Coins that are in excellent condition, with sharp details, original surfaces, and no wear, are graded as "Mint State" or "Uncirculated" and are generally the most valuable. Coins that are well-worn or damaged, with few details visible or significant scratches or other blemishes, are graded as "About Good" or "Poor" and are typically worth much less. In addition to wearing and damage, other factors that can affect the condition of a coin include toning, cleaning, and other alterations. Coins that have been cleaned or otherwise altered in some way may be worth less than similar coins that have not been altered, as these modifications can affect the coin's appearance and reduce its desirability among collectors.

Demand:

Finally, the demand for a particular coin can also affect its value. If a particular coin is popular among collectors, its value may increase as more people try to acquire it. Demand is a crucial factor in assessing the value of a coin. Coins that are rare or difficult to find are often in high demand and can command high prices in the coin market. Similarly, coins that have played an important role in history or that are associated with famous people or events are often in high demand and can be highly sought after by collectors.

The popularity of a particular type of coin can also affect its value. For example, coins that are part of a popular collection, such as a series of coins produced by a particular mint, can be highly valued by collectors who are interested in completing their collection. Similarly, coins that have a particular aesthetic appeal, such as those with intricate designs or unusual shapes, can be highly valued by collectors who appreciate these features. The level of demand for a coin can be influenced by a variety of other factors, such as economic conditions, changes in collector preferences, and the availability of similar coins in the market.

Coins that are in high demand are typically more valuable than coins that are not in demand, even if they are relatively common or not particularly rare or historically significant. There are many resources available to help collectors determine the value of their coins, including coin grading guides, price guides, and online marketplaces where coins are bought and sold. It's important to do research and consult multiple sources when evaluating the value of a particular coin, as values can vary depending on the market and other factors.

Book 3:
Avoiding Forgeries And Counterfeits

As with any collectible item, coins are also vulnerable to forgeries and counterfeits. With advances in technology and techniques, it has become increasingly challenging to detect fake coins, making it more critical than ever to learn how to identify and avoid them. In this book, we will explore the various types of coin forgeries and counterfeits, from ancient coins to modern-day issues, and the methods used to produce them. We'll also discuss the different tools and techniques used to detect counterfeit coins, including visual inspection, weight and size measurements, and chemical analysis. By the end of this book, you will have a comprehensive understanding of the types of coin forgeries and counterfeits and the steps you can take to protect your coin collection from fraud.

Chapter 1:
Understanding Fake And Counterfeit Coins

Fake and counterfeit coins are imitations of genuine coins that are made with the intention to deceive and defraud collectors, investors, and other individuals. These coins can be difficult to detect, and they can have serious consequences for those who unknowingly purchase them. There are several different types of fake and counterfeit coins, including:

Counterfeit coins:

Counterfeit coins are coins that are made to resemble genuine coins but are not produced by an authorized mint and are made with the intention to deceive and defraud collectors, investors, and other individuals. Counterfeit coins can be made from base metals or other materials and are often produced using modern technology and sophisticated techniques that make them difficult to detect. Counterfeiters often target coins that are rare or have significant historical or cultural value, as these coins can be highly valuable and are in high demand among collectors and investors. They may also produce counterfeit coins that are part of popular collections, such as those produced by particular mints or that have certain aesthetic or design features.

Altered coins:

Altered coins are genuine coins that have been modified or manipulated in some way to make them appear more valuable or rare than they actually are. Altered coins can include coins that have been engraved, polished, cleaned, or otherwise modified in an attempt to improve their appearance or make them more desirable to collectors and investors. Some common examples of altered coins include:

Re-engraved coins: Re-engraved coins are genuine coins that have been altered by adding a new date or mintmark through engraving or other techniques. Re-engraved coins are a type of altered coin and can be difficult to detect, especially if the re-engraving is well-executed and the new date or mintmark is similar in style to the original. Re-engraved coins are often produced by individuals or groups with the intention of deceiving collectors and investors. The re-engraving is done to make the coin appear more valuable or rare than it actually is, and it can significantly increase the value of the coin if the deception is not detected.

To detect a re-engraved coin, there are several things to look for. First, examine the date and mintmark closely and compare them to other examples of the same coin. The new date or mintmark may appear different in style, size, or placement compared to the original. Additionally, the surfaces of the coin around the area where the re-engraving was done may appear differently than the rest of the coin due to the use of different tools or techniques.

It's important to note that re-engraving a coin is illegal in many jurisdictions, and owning or selling re-engraved coins can have legal consequences. It's always recommended to purchase coins from reputable dealers who can provide information on the authenticity and history of the coin. If you suspect that a coin you own or are considering purchasing has been re-engraved, you should have it examined by a professional coin appraiser or grading service to confirm its authenticity and condition.

Polished or cleaned coins:

Polished or cleaned coins are genuine coins that have been altered by removing surface blemishes, dirt, or other imperfections to improve their appearance. While cleaning a coin may seem like a good idea to make it look better, it can actually damage the coin and significantly decrease its value. Cleaning a coin can cause scratches, hairlines, and other types of damage to the surface of the coin, which can reduce its condition and grade. In addition, cleaning can also remove the natural toning or patina that forms on a coin over time, which is an important part of the coin's history and can affect its value. To detect a polished or cleaned coin, look for signs of polishing or damage on the high points of the coin's design, such as letters or images. A cleaned or polished coin will often have a shiny or reflective surface, and the details of the design may be less sharp or distinct than on an uncleaned coin.

It's important to note that professional coin graders and appraisers can easily detect cleaning or polishing, and coins that have been cleaned or polished will receive lower grades and be worth less than coins in their original, uncleaned condition. To preserve the value of your coins, it's best to avoid cleaning them altogether. If you need to handle your coins, be sure to use clean, soft materials that won't scratch or damage the surface. And if you're purchasing coins, be sure to buy from reputable dealers who can provide information on the coin's condition and history.

Counter-stamped coins:

Counter-stamped coins are genuine coins that have been stamped with a new design or symbol, often by a private mint or individual, to create a unique and personalized item. Counter-stamping was a common practice in the past when coins were used as a form of currency, and merchants would often add their own mark to coins to denote their authenticity or origin. Counter-stamped coins can also be created by collectors or investors as a way to enhance the value of a coin or create a unique collectible item. These counter-stamped coins can include the date, mintmark, initials of the creator, or other designs and symbols that are meaningful or significant to the owner.

It's important to note that counter-stamping a coin can significantly affect its value, both positively and negatively. If the counter-stamping is done in a way that enhances the historical significance or rarity of the coin, it can increase its value to collectors and investors. On the other hand, if the counter-stamping is done in a way that damages or alters the original design of the coin, it can decrease its value and authenticity. To detect a counter-stamped coin, examine the coin closely for any additional marks or symbols that were not part of the original design. Look for differences in style, size, or placement compared to the original design, and consider the historical significance of the counter stamp. If you're considering purchasing a counter-stamped coin, be sure to do your research and buy from a reputable dealer who can provide information on the coin's condition, history, and authenticity.

Altered coins can be difficult to detect, and collectors and investors should be careful when purchasing coins that have been altered in any way. It is important to buy coins from reputable dealers and to do your research before making a purchase. Look for coins that are certified by reputable grading services, like the Professional Coin Grading Service or the Numismatic Guaranty Corporation, and be wary of coins that are being sold at prices that seem too good to be true. If you suspect that a coin you own or are considering purchasing has been altered, you should have it examined by a professional coin appraiser or grading service to confirm its authenticity and condition. This can help you avoid making a costly mistake and ensure that you are purchasing genuine coins for your collection or investment portfolio.

Replicas:

A replica coin is a copy or reproduction of a genuine coin, often made to look like the original. Replica coins can be made for a variety of reasons, such as for educational purposes, to fill a gap in a collection, or as souvenirs or decorations. Replica coins can be made from a variety of materials, including metals, plastics, or other materials that can mimic the look and feel of the original coin. While replica coins are not genuine, they can still be interesting and valuable to collectors or historians as examples of the design or historical significance of a particular coin.

It's important to note that replica coins are not legal tender and should not be sold or used as if they were genuine coins. Additionally, some jurisdictions have laws that regulate the production and sale of replica coins, so it's important to check the legality of owning or selling replicas in your area. When purchasing a replica coin, be sure to buy from a reputable dealer who can provide information on the origin, materials, and condition of the replica. Additionally, it's important to be aware of the differences between the replica and the genuine coin, as well as any markings or indicators that denote it as a replica, to avoid any confusion or misrepresentation.

To avoid purchasing fake or counterfeit coins, it is important to buy coins from reputable dealers and to do your research before making a purchase. If you suspect that a coin you own or are considering purchasing is fake or counterfeit, you should have it examined by a professional coin appraiser or grading service to confirm its authenticity. This can help you avoid making a costly mistake and ensure that you are purchasing genuine coins for your collection or investment portfolio.

Chapter 2:
How To Identify A Forged Coin

Forgeries have been a part of the coin-collecting world for almost as long as coins have been in circulation. The rise of advanced technology and easy access to information has made it easier for fraudsters to create convincing fake coins that can fool even experienced collectors. The ability to identify a forged coin is crucial for anyone interested in coin collecting, as the purchase of a fake coin can result in financial loss and damage to a collector's reputation. This chapter will provide a comprehensive guide to identifying a forged coin, covering the key characteristics and indicators to look for when evaluating a coin's authenticity. Whether you are a seasoned collector or just starting out, this guide will help you avoid the pitfalls of fake coins and make informed decisions about building and maintaining your collection. However, there are several things you can look for to help determine whether a coin is genuine or fake:

Weight and size:

One of the most obvious indicators of a forged coin is a difference in weight or size compared to a genuine coin. If you have access to a genuine coin to compare it to, weigh and measure both coins to see if there are any significant differences. To check the weight and size of a coin, you will need a precise scale and calipers, which are tools used for measuring small distances. Here are the steps to check the weight and size of a coin:

Place the coin on the scale and note its weight. If you have a genuine coin to compare it to, weigh both coins to see if there are any significant differences. Make sure to use a suitable scale that is accurate to at least 0.01 grams for smaller coins and up to 0.1 grams for larger coins.

Use calipers to measure the diameter of the coin. Place the calipers on opposite sides of the coin's edge and gently close them until they touch the coin. Take note of the measurement in millimeters.

If the coin has a reeded edge, you can use the calipers to measure the number of reeds on the circumference of the coin. Simply count the number of reeds over a short distance, such as 10mm, and compare it to the number of reeds on a genuine coin.

It's important to note that some counterfeit coins may have the correct weight and size but still be fake due to other factors, such as the design or materials used. Therefore, it's always a good idea to have a suspected counterfeit coin examined by a professional coin appraiser or grading service to confirm its authenticity.

Edge lettering:

Many modern coins have lettering or other designs on the edge of the coin that can be difficult to replicate. Check the edge of the coin for any irregularities or inconsistencies in the lettering or design. o check the edge lettering of a coin, you will need a magnifying glass or loupe, which is a small magnifying lens. Here are the steps to check the edge lettering of a coin:

Hold the coin by its edge, with the obverse (front) facing up and the reverse (back) facing down.

Use the magnifying glass or loupe to examine the edge of the coin closely. Look for any lettering or designs that are present on the edge of the coin.

Compare the edge lettering to a known genuine coin of the same type, if possible. Look for any differences or inconsistencies in the lettering or design.

Check for the correct orientation of the edge lettering. In some cases, edge lettering may be upside down or oriented in the wrong direction on counterfeit coins.

It's important to note that not all coins have edge lettering, so this method may not be applicable to all coins. Additionally, some counterfeit coins may have edge lettering that is difficult to distinguish from genuine lettering, so it's always a good idea to have a suspected counterfeit coin examined by a professional coin appraiser or grading service to confirm its authenticity.

Details of the design:

Examine the details of the coin's design closely to look for any differences or inconsistencies compared to a genuine coin. Forgers may have difficulty replicating the intricate details of a coin's design, resulting in slight variations or mistakes. To check the details of the design of a coin, you will need a magnifying glass or loupe, which is a small magnifying lens. Here are the steps to check the details of the design of a coin:

Hold the coin by its edge, with the obverse (front) facing up and the reverse (back) facing down.

Use the magnifying glass or loupe to examine the design of the coin closely. Look for any differences or inconsistencies compared to a genuine coin of the same type.

Check for any variations in the design, such as missing or extra details or differences in the size or shape of certain elements.

Look for any signs of wear or damage, which could indicate that the coin has been altered or tampered with.

Check for any signs of artificial toning or colorization, which can be a sign of a counterfeit coin.

It's important to note that some counterfeit coins may be very well made and difficult to distinguish from genuine coins based on design alone. Therefore, it's always a good idea to have a suspected counterfeit coin examined by a professional coin appraiser or grading service to confirm its authenticity.

Magnetism:

Some counterfeit coins may be made of materials that are attracted to magnets, which genuine coins are not. Use a magnet to test the coin to see if it is magnetic. To check the magnetism of a coin, you will need a magnet. Here are the steps to check the magnetism of a coin:

Hold the magnet close to the coin and see if it is attracted to the magnet. A genuine coin should not be attracted to a magnet, as most coins are made from non-magnetic metals such as copper, nickel, or silver. If the coin is attracted to the magnet, it may be a counterfeit made from a magnetic metal such as iron, steel, or cobalt.

Additionally, some counterfeit coins may be non-magnetic or have magnetic properties that are difficult to detect with a simple magnet test. Therefore, it's always a good idea to have a suspected counterfeit coin examined by a professional coin appraiser or grading service to confirm its authenticity.

Sound:

Genuine coins have a distinctive sound when they are dropped or tapped, which can be difficult to replicate. If you have access to a genuine coin, compare the sound it makes to the sound of the coin in question. To check a coin by sound, you will need to tap or drop the coin onto a hard surface, such as a table or a desk. Here are the steps to check a coin by sound:

Hold the coin by its edge, with the obverse (front) facing up and the reverse (back) facing down.

Tap the edge of the coin gently against a hard surface, such as a table or a desk. Listen to the sound that the coin makes.

A genuine coin should produce a clear, ringing sound when it is tapped, with a consistent tone and duration.

If the sound is dull or muted, it may be a sign that the coin is made from a base metal or has been tampered with.

Some counterfeit coins may be made from a different metal or have a different composition than a genuine coin, which can affect the sound that they make when tapped. However, this method can be a useful way to identify certain types of counterfeit coins, particularly those made from base metals or other materials that do not produce a clear, ringing sound.

Microscopic examination:

Advanced techniques such as microscopic examination can reveal the fine details of a coin's design and surface, which can help identify a forgery. Microscopic examination is a useful method for identifying counterfeit coins and detecting signs of alteration or tampering. Here are the steps to check a coin by microscopic examination:

- Use a high-powered microscope or a specialized tool such as a stereo microscope to examine the surface of the coin.
- Look for any signs of tool marks or surface damage, which could indicate that the coin has been altered or tampered with.

- Check the edge of the coin for signs of reed marks or other details, which should be sharp and well-defined on a genuine coin.
- Examine the design of the coin for any signs of variation or inconsistency, such as missing or extra details or differences in the size or shape of certain elements.
- Check for any signs of artificial toning or colorization, which can be a sign of a counterfeit coin.
- Examine the surface of the coin for any signs of casting or plating marks, which could indicate that the coin is a fake.
- If the coin has been encapsulated or graded, examine the holder or label for signs of tampering or alteration.

Microscopic examination can be a highly effective way to detect counterfeit coins, as it can reveal subtle differences in the surface of the coin that is difficult to detect with the naked eye. However, it requires specialized equipment and expertise, so it's best to have a professional coin appraiser or grading service perform this type of examination.

If you suspect a coin is forged, it's important to have it examined by a professional coin appraiser or grading service. These experts can use specialized equipment and knowledge to help determine the coin's authenticity and value.

Chapter 3:
Prevention Techniques To Avoid Scams

Coin scams are a prevalent problem in the industry, and they can take many forms, including counterfeit coins, over-graded coins, and misrepresented coins. The effects of falling prey to coin scams can be devastating, not only financially but also in terms of the collector's confidence and trust in the industry. In this chapter, we will explore various prevention techniques that collectors can use to avoid falling victim to coin scams. We'll discuss strategies such as conducting thorough research, buying from reputable dealers, and understanding grading standards. By the end of this chapter, you will have a comprehensive understanding of the best practices to protect yourself from coin scams and make informed decisions when adding to your collection. Here are some prevention techniques to avoid coin scams:

Buy from reputable dealers: When buying coins, make sure to buy from reputable and trusted dealers. Do some research and read reviews to ensure that the dealer is reputable and has a good track record of selling authentic coins. Here are some tips on how to buy coins from reputable dealers:

Attend coin shows: Coin shows are a great way to meet reputable dealers and see their inventory in person. Attend local coin shows to meet dealers and learn more about the coins you are interested in.

Ask for references: Ask the dealer for references from other customers or collectors. Reputable dealers will be happy to provide references and reviews from satisfied customers.

Check their credentials: Check if the dealer is a member of professional institutes, such as the PNG or ANA. These organizations have strict codes of ethics and require members to meet certain standards of professionalism.

Inspect the coin: When you have found a coin you are interested in, inspect it carefully. Look for any signs of wear, damage, or alteration. Reputable dealers will be transparent about the condition and authenticity of the coins they are selling.

Understand their return policy: Reputable dealers will have a clear return policy and will stand behind the coins they sell. Make sure you understand the dealer's return policy before making a purchase.

Find a professional appraiser: Look for a professional appraiser who specializes in the type of coins you are interested in. The American Numismatic Association-ANA and the Professional Numismatists Guild-PNG, both offer directories of professional appraisers.

Attend coin shows: Coin shows are a great place to meet appraisers and get a second opinion on a coin you are interested in. Many shows have experts available to offer opinions and appraisals.

Use online grading services: There are several online grading services that can provide an independent assessment of a coin's condition and authenticity. These services can be a good way to get a second opinion without having to physically bring the coin to an appraiser.

Be cautious of biased opinions: When getting a second opinion, be cautious of biased opinions. Some dealers or appraisers may have a vested interest in the sale of the coin, so it's important to get opinions from multiple sources. By getting a second opinion before buying coins, you can ensure that you are making an informed decision and getting the best value for your money.

Do your research: Educate yourself about the coins you are interested in and learn about the various factors that affect their value, such as mintage, condition, and rarity.

Verify authenticity: Always verify the authenticity of a coin before making a purchase. Use reputable grading services or seek the opinion of a professional appraiser to ensure that the coin is genuine.

Be wary of high-pressure sales tactics: Scammers often use high-pressure sales tactics to make you feel like you need to act quickly to secure a good deal. Take your time and do your due diligence before making a purchase.

Use a trusted payment method: Use a payment method that offers buyer protection, such as PayPal or a credit card. Avoid sending cash or using wire transfers, as these methods are difficult to track and offer little protection in case of a scam. By being wary of "too good to be true" coin deals, you can protect yourself from scams and ensure that you are making informed purchases.

Inspect the coin before you buy: Carefully inspect the coin before you buy it. Look for any signs of wear, damage, or tampering, and check for any inconsistencies or variations in the design.

Avoid buying from unverified sources: Yes, it's important to avoid buying coins from unverified sources, as this increases the risk of purchasing counterfeit or altered coins. Here are some tips to help you avoid buying coins from unverified sources:

Research the seller:

Before making a purchase, research the seller to ensure that they have a good reputation in the numismatic community. Look for reviews and ratings on online marketplaces, or ask for references from other collectors.

Verify the seller's credentials:

Verify the seller's credentials and memberships in numismatic organizations. The American Numismatic Association-ANA and the Professional Numismatists Guild-PNG, both offer directories of reputable dealers.

Be wary of private sellers:

Be cautious when dealing with private sellers, especially those who are not well-known in the numismatic community. It's often best to purchase from reputable dealers who are knowledgeable and experienced in the field.

Avoid buying from unknown websites:

Be cautious when purchasing coins from unknown websites. Stick with well-established and reputable online marketplaces or dealer websites that have a track record of providing quality service and authentic coins.

Get a certificate of authenticity:

Always request a certificate of authenticity for any coin you purchase, especially if it's a high-value coin. This document will verify the coin's authenticity and provide important information about its history and condition.

By avoiding unverified sources and purchasing from reputable dealers or online marketplaces, you can reduce the risk of purchasing counterfeit or altered coins and ensure that you are getting authentic coins at a fair price.

Book 4:
Protecting Your Coin Collection

A coin collection can also be a valuable investment that can provide financial security for years to come. However, a coin collection is not without risks. Coins can be lost, stolen, or damaged, and the consequences can be devastating. In this book, we will explore the various ways to protect your coin collection, from safe storage and insurance to security measures and disaster preparedness. We'll discuss the most common risks that coin collectors face and provide practical tips and strategies to mitigate those risks. By the end of this book, you will have a comprehensive understanding of how to protect your coin collection and ensure that it remains safe, secure, and valuable for years to come.

Chapter 1:
Best Practices For Collecting Coins

Coin collecting is a fascinating hobby that requires a combination of knowledge, passion, and skill. Whether you are a beginner or an experienced collector, there are certain best practices that you can follow to make the most of your collection. In this chapter, we will explore some of the essential best practices for collecting coins, from setting goals and budgets to expanding your knowledge and network. We'll discuss the importance of conducting research, creating a wish list, and understanding grading standards. We'll also talk about the value of networking with other collectors and professionals in the industry. By the end of this chapter, you will have a comprehensive understanding of the best practices for collecting coins and how to apply them to your own collection.

Chapter 2:
Proper Handling And Storage Techniques

Proper handling and storage techniques are crucial for maintaining the value and condition of coins. Coins are not just pieces of metal, but they also represent historical and cultural significance. It is essential to handle and store coins carefully to prevent any damage, wear, or corrosion that can reduce their numismatic value. In this chapter, we will discuss the proper handling and storage techniques for coins, including how to handle coins, the tools and equipment necessary for coin handling, and the best practices for storing coins to keep them in excellent condition. Whether you are a collector, dealer, or simply someone who values coins, this chapter will provide you with the essential knowledge and skills to ensure that your coins remain in pristine condition. Here are some tips for handling and storing coins:

Hold coins by their edges: When handling coins, hold them by their edges or rims rather than touching the surface. This will help prevent scratches, fingerprints, and other damage.

Use coin holders: Use coin holders, such as coin flips, coin capsules, or coin albums, to protect your coins from damage and prevent contact with other coins. Choose holders made of materials that won't damage the coins, such as acid-free paper or plastic.

Store coins in a cool, dry place: Store your coins in a cool, dry place, away from direct sunlight, moisture, and fluctuations in temperature. Avoid storing coins in areas that are subject to extreme temperatures, such as attics or basements.

Avoid using staples or paperclips: When storing coins in cardboard holders or flips, avoid using staples or paperclips, as they can damage the coins. Instead, use adhesive tape or mylar strips to secure the holders. It is important to avoid using staples or paperclips when storing coins, as they can damage the coins and decrease their value. Here's why:

Scratches: Staples and paperclips can scratch the surface of the coins when they come into contact with them. Scratches can decrease the coin's value and make it less appealing to collectors.

Tarnishing: Staples and paperclips can also cause tarnishing on the surface of the coin. This is especially true if the clips are made of metal, as they can react with the metal in the coin and cause corrosion.

Bending: The use of staples or paperclips can cause the coin holder to bend or warp, which can cause damage to the coin inside. This is especially true for thin cardboard holders, which can easily bend and become misshapen. Bending coins is generally not recommended, as it can damage the coins and decrease their value. Here are some reasons why bending coins is not a good idea:

Damage to the coin's surface: Bending a coin can cause damage to the surface of the coin, such as scratches, dings, or nicks. These imperfections can significantly reduce the coin's value and make it less appealing to collectors.

Altering the coin's shape: Bending a coin can also alter its shape, which can cause it to be considered "damaged" by coin grading companies. Altered coins are generally worth much less than their original, unaltered counterparts.

Decreased historical or artistic value: Coins are often valued for their historical or artistic significance, and bending a coin can damage or alter these important features. In extreme cases, bending a coin can completely destroy its historical or artistic value.

Legal issues: In some cases, intentionally damaging or defacing a coin can be illegal. While this is not true for all countries, it's important to be aware of the laws in your area before altering a coin in any way.

Label coin holders: If you are storing multiple coins in the same holder, label each holder with the date, mint mark, and other pertinent information to prevent confusion and ensure easy identification. Labeling coin holders is a useful practice to keep your coins organized and properly identified. Here are some tips for labeling your coin holders:

- When labeling coin holders, use a permanent marker with archival-quality ink that won't smudge or fade over time. Avoid using a ballpoint pen, which can scratch the surface of the coin holder or fade over time.

- Label each coin holder with important information about the coin, such as the date, mint mark, denomination, and any other identifying features. You may also want to include the grade or condition of the coin, if applicable.
- Use a consistent format for labeling your coin holders, such as writing the date first, followed by the mint mark and denomination. This will help ensure that your coins are easily identified and organized.
- To save space on the label, use abbreviations for common terms, such as "P" for Philadelphia, "D" for Denver, and "S" for San Francisco's mint.
- While it's important to label your coin holders, avoid over-labeling, as this can make it difficult to read the information. Use a clear and concise format for labeling your coin holders to keep them easy to read and organized.

By labeling your coin holders with important information, you can easily identify and organize your coins, making it easier to manage your collection and keep track of valuable pieces.

Chapter 3:
Caring For And Cleaning Your Coins

Caring for and cleaning your coins is a crucial aspect of coin collecting and investment. Coins are made of different metals and can be easily damaged, corroded, or discolored if not handled and cleaned properly. However, with the right knowledge and tools, cleaning and caring for your coins can significantly enhance their value and appearance. In this chapter, we will explore the techniques, tools, and best practices for cleaning and caring for your coins, including how to identify different types of coins, how to handle them safely, and how to clean them without causing damage. Whether you are a novice collector or an experienced numismatist, the information in this chapter will provide you with the essential skills to preserve your coins' condition and value. Here are some tips for caring for and cleaning your coins:

- Handling coins carefully is important to prevent damage and preserve their value. Here are some tips for handling coins carefully:
- Before handling coins, it is important to wash your hands thoroughly with soap and water. This will remove any oils or dirt on your hands that can damage the coins.
- When picking up a coin, avoid touching the face of the coin. Instead, hold it by the edges, using your thumb and forefinger.
- If you are handling valuable coins or coins that are particularly delicate, it may be best to wear gloves to prevent fingerprints or other marks from damaging the coin.
- Rubbing or cleaning coins can cause scratches or other damage that can reduce their value. If you need to clean a coin, use a soft, lint-free cloth and only use water or a coin-cleaning solution specifically designed for coins.

Coin Cleaning:

Cleaning coins is generally not recommended, as it can reduce their value and damage their surface. However, if you have coins that are heavily soiled or tarnished and you want to clean them, there are some methods you can use:

Warm water and mild soap: Gently clean the coin with a soft-bristled toothbrush and warm water with a small amount of mild soap. Rinse the coin thoroughly and pat dry with a soft cloth.

Baking soda paste method: Mix baking soda with water to make a paste, and lightly brush it on the coin. Gently rub the paste onto the surface of the coin with a soft-bristled toothbrush, and then rinse it thoroughly with water. Pat dry with a soft cloth.

Lemon juice: Soak the coin in lemon juice for a few minutes, and then gently scrub it with a soft-bristled toothbrush. Rinse the coin thoroughly with water and pat dry with a soft cloth.

Vinegar: Soak the coin in vinegar for a few minutes, and then gently scrub it with a soft-bristled toothbrush. Rinse the coin thoroughly with water and pat dry with a soft cloth.

Remember, cleaning coins can reduce their value and damage their surface, so it is generally best to leave them as they are, especially if they have any historical or collector value. If you are unsure about the best method to use or if the coin is especially valuable, it is recommended to consult with a professional coin dealer or conservationist.

Coin Storage

Proper storage is important to prevent damage to coins. Store coins in individual coin holders or coin albums, and keep them in a dry, cool place away from direct sunlight.

Use individual coin holders or coin albums: Coins should be stored individually in coin holders or coin albums to prevent them from rubbing against each other and getting scratched. Coin holders and albums can be made of various materials, such as cardboard, plastic, or Mylar, and come in various sizes and shapes to accommodate different coin types and sizes.

Keep coins in a dry and cool place: Moisture and heat can damage coins, so it's essential to keep them in a dry and cool place, away from direct sunlight, humidity, and extreme temperatures. A coin safe or a bank safety deposit box can be a good option to protect your coins from environmental factors.

Avoid storing coins in containers with PVC: Polyvinyl chloride (PVC) can release acidic gases that can cause damage to coins over time. Therefore, it's essential to avoid storing coins in containers with PVC or plasticizers.

Label and organize your coins: Labeling and organizing your coins can help you keep track of your collection, making it easier to locate specific coins and keep an inventory. You can use labels, tags, or a detailed inventory system to keep track of your collection.

Avoid cleaning valuable coins: If you have valuable coins, it's best to avoid cleaning them altogether. Any cleaning can potentially damage the coin and reduce its value. If you need to determine the authenticity or condition of a valuable coin, consult a professional coin appraiser or grading service.

Overall, the key to caring for and cleaning your coins is to handle them carefully and avoid any harsh or abrasive methods that could cause damage. With proper care, your coins can remain in excellent condition for years to come.

Chapter 4:
Common Causes Of Damage To Coins

Coins are fascinating artifacts that tell stories of history and culture. As collectibles and investments, coins must be treated with care and respect to maintain their value and condition. Unfortunately, coins can be easily damaged, resulting in reduced numismatic value. In this chapter, we will explore the common causes of damage to coins, including factors that can lead to wear, corrosion, and other forms of damage. By understanding the causes of damage, collectors and investors can take proactive measures to prevent damage to their coin collections. We will also discuss the types of damage that can occur and the impact they can have on a coin's value. Whether you are a seasoned numismatist or a beginner collector, this chapter will provide valuable insights into protecting your coin collection. Here are some of the most common causes of damage to coins:

Environmental damage:

Exposure to air, moisture, and other environmental elements can cause damage to coins. This can include oxidation, tarnishing, and corrosion. Oxidation: Exposure to air can cause coins to oxidize and develop a greenish or brownish patina. This can reduce the value of the coin and make it less attractive to collectors.

Tarnishing: Exposure to moisture can cause coins to tarnish and develop a dull, grayish appearance. This can also reduce the value of the coin and make it less attractive to collectors.

Corrosion: Exposure to moisture, acids, and other environmental factors can cause coins to corrode and develop pitting or other types of damage. This can be especially damaging to coins made from metals like copper or silver. To prevent environmental damage to your coins, it's important to store them in a cool, dry place, preferably in an acid-free holder or album. Coins should be kept away from moisture and other environmental factors and should be handled with clean, dry hands to prevent oils and other contaminants from coming into contact with the coin's surface.

Mishandling:

Rough handling of coins can cause scratches, dents, and other types of damage. This can be caused by dropping the coin, rubbing it against hard surfaces, or other types of physical impact. Mishandling is another common cause of damage to coins. Some of the most common types of mishandling that can damage coins include:

Dropping the coin: Dropping a coin can cause it to suffer dents, scratches, and other types of physical damage.

Rubbing against hard surfaces: Rubbing a coin against a hard surface, such as a table or countertop, can cause scratches and other types of physical damage.

Cleaning the coin with harsh chemicals: Cleaning coins with harsh chemicals or abrasive materials can cause damage to the surface of the coin.

Fingers and other contaminants: Touching the surface of a coin with fingers or other contaminants can leave oils and another residue on the surface of the coin, which can cause damage over time.

To prevent mishandling damage to your coins, it's important to handle them with care. Coins should be stored in protective holders or albums to prevent accidental drops or to rub against hard surfaces. When handling a coin, it's important to hold it by the edges and to avoid touching the surface of the coin with your fingers or other contaminants. If you need to clean a coin, it's important to use only gentle cleaning methods and to avoid using harsh chemicals or abrasive materials.

Improper storage:

Improper storage of coins can cause damage that can reduce their value. Here are some ways that improper storage can damage coins:

Scratches and abrasions: Coins that are stored improperly can rub against each other or against other objects, causing scratches, abrasions, and other damage to the surface of the coin. This can reduce the coin's value and make it less desirable to collectors.

Tarnishing and corrosion: Exposure to air, moisture, and other environmental factors can cause coins to tarnish or corrode, which can also reduce their value.

Chemical damage: Some materials, such as PVC or other plastics, can release chemicals that can damage coins over time. Coins that are stored in these materials can develop discoloration or other forms of chemical damage.

Fading: Exposure to sunlight or other sources of UV radiation can cause the colors on some coins, such as proof coins or commemorative coins, to fade over time.

To avoid damage from improper storage, it's essential to store your coins in individual coin holders or albums in a dry and cool place, away from direct sunlight, humidity, and extreme temperatures. Avoid storing coins in containers with PVC or other materials that can release chemicals that can damage coins. By storing your coins properly, you can help preserve their condition and value for years to come.

Chemical damage:

Chemical damage to coins can occur when they are exposed to substances such as acids, oils, or cleaning agents that can react with the metal and cause corrosion or discoloration. To prevent chemical damage to coins, you can take the following steps:

Handle coins carefully: When handling coins, avoid touching them with your bare hands, as the oils and acids from your skin can cause damage. Use gloves or hold coins by their edges to prevent direct contact.

Store coins in protective holders: Store coins in acid-free, archival-quality holders or albums that will protect them from exposure to air, moisture, and chemicals.

Avoid harsh cleaning agents: Never use harsh cleaning agents or abrasive materials to clean coins, as they can cause chemical damage. Stick to the gentle cleaning methods mentioned in the previous answer.

Keep coins away from harmful substances: Keep coins away from substances that can cause chemical damage, such as PVC plastic, which can release harmful chemicals that can react with the coin's metal. Store coins in holders or albums that are made from materials that are safe for coin storage.

By taking these steps, you can help to prevent chemical damage to your coins and keep them in good condition for years to come. If you are unsure about the best way to store or handle your coins, or if you suspect that they may have been damaged, it is recommended to consult with a professional coin dealer or conservationist.

Circulation: The circulation of coins refers to the process by which coins are distributed and used as a means of payment in everyday transactions. In most countries, the circulation of coins is managed by the central bank, which is responsible for producing and distributing the country's currency.

Coins typically enter circulation through banks, which order them from the central bank to meet the demand for coins from businesses and consumers. Once in circulation, coins can be used to make purchases and payments, and they may change hands many times before eventually being returned to a bank or the central bank. Over time, coins can become worn or damaged from repeated use, and they may need to be replaced with new coins. The central bank periodically withdraws worn or damaged coins from circulation and replaces them with new coins, a process known as coin recycling.

The circulation of coins is an important aspect of the monetary system, as it provides a means of exchange that is widely accepted and trusted by the public. By managing the supply of coins and ensuring their quality, the central bank helps to support the economy and facilitate commerce. To prevent damage to your coins, it's important to handle them carefully, store them properly, and avoid exposing them to environmental or chemical factors that can cause damage.

Chapter 5:
Understanding Mint Coins

Mint coins are coins that are produced by a government mint, usually on behalf of the country's central bank. The minting process involves creating the design for the coin, striking the blank metal discs (known as planchets) with the design using a coining press, and then finishing and packaging the coins for distribution. Mint coins are generally considered to be of higher quality and value than other types of coins due to the strict quality control measures that are in place during the minting process. Mint coins are typically uncirculated, which means they have not been used in daily commerce and are free from the wear and tear that occurs during circulation. Some popular examples of mint coins include:

Bullion coins: These are coins that are made of precious metals and are primarily used for investment purposes.

Commemorative coins: These are coins that are issued to commemorate a significant event, such as an anniversary or the opening of a new monument or building.

Proof coins: These are specially made coins that have a high level of detail and finish and are produced using a special minting process. Proof coins are often sold as collectors' items and are highly valued due to their rarity and quality.

Limited edition coins: These are coins that are produced in limited quantities and often high in demand.

Overall, mint coins are a popular choice for investors and collectors due to their quality, rarity, and historical significance. When purchasing mint coins, it's important to buy from reputable dealers and to verify the authenticity and quality of the coins through third-party grading services.

Book 5:
Monetizing Your Coin Collection

Monetizing your coin collection requires a good understanding of the market, the value of your coins, and the different options for selling your coins. In this book, we will provide a comprehensive guide to monetizing your coin collection, covering a range of topics such as the different types of coin values, determining the value of your coins, grading, and authentication, and the various options for selling your coins, including auctions, dealers, and online marketplaces. Whether you are looking to sell your entire collection or just a few select coins, this book will provide you with the knowledge and skills to get the most out of your investment.

Chapter 1:
Essential Considerations Before Investing In Coins

Investing in coins can be an exciting and rewarding venture, but it is essential to approach it with caution and care. Coin investments are not without risk, and novice investors can make costly mistakes if they do not have a good understanding of the market and the key factors that affect coin values. In this chapter, we will explore the essential considerations that every investor should be aware of before investing in coins. We will cover topics such as understanding the coin market, identifying different types of coins, grading and authentication, and the potential risks and rewards of coin investing. By understanding these critical considerations, investors can make informed decisions and maximize their returns while minimizing their risks. Whether you are a seasoned investor or new to the world of coin collecting, the information in this chapter will provide a solid foundation for successful coin investing. Here are some essential considerations to keep in mind before investing in coins:

Research:

Before investing in coins, do your research to gain a good understanding of the market, the different types of coins available, and the factors that can affect their value. Look for reliable sources of information, such as reputable coin dealers, auction houses, and publications. Researching the coin market is an important step in making informed decisions when investing in coins. Here are some ways to research the coin market:

Industry publications:

Industry publications, such as Coin World and Numismatic News, provide information on the latest trends, market reports, and upcoming auctions. Subscribing to these publications can help you stay up to date with the latest news and information in the coin market.

Auction houses:

Heritage Auctions or Stack's Bowers Galleries are an example of auction houses, and they offer a wealth of information on the coin market, including prices realized for recently sold coins and upcoming auctions. You can also attend auctions or view them online to see what types of coins are in demand and selling for high prices.

Coin dealers:

Experienced coin dealers can provide valuable insights into the coin market, as they are knowledgeable about current market conditions and can help you assess the value and authenticity of coins. Look for reputable dealers who have a good track record of customer service and sales.

Online marketplaces:

Online marketplaces, such as eBay and Amazon, can be useful resources for researching the coin market. You can view current listings and prices for a wide range of coins and read reviews from other buyers and sellers.

Numismatic associations:

Numismatic associations, like ANA and the PNG, offer resources and information on the coin market, as well as networking opportunities with other collectors and dealers.

Historical data:

Historical data on coin prices and market trends can be useful for assessing the performance of the coin market over time. You can find historical data on coin prices from sources such as the Coin Dealer Newsletter and the Professional Coin Grading Service. By conducting thorough research on the coin market, you can gain a better understanding of current market conditions and make more informed decisions when investing in coins.

Quality:

The quality of a coin can have a significant impact on its value, so it is important to pay attention to factors such as grade, condition, and authenticity. Invest in coins that are graded by a reputable third-party grading company and authenticated by a recognized expert in the field.

Rarity:

Coins that are rare or have a low mintage can be highly sought after by collectors and can command a premium price. Look for coins that have a limited availability or historical significance, as these may be more likely to increase in value over time.

Liquidity:

Consider the ease with which you can sell your coins if you need to liquidate your investment. Look for coins that are popular and in high demand, as these are likely to be more easily sellable in the future.

Budget:

Set a budget for your coin investment and stick to it. Avoid investing more than you can afford to lose, and be prepared to hold onto your coins for the long term to allow their value to appreciate.

Storage:

Invest in proper storage and protection for your coins to preserve their quality and value. Consider investing in a safe or safety deposit box to keep your coins secure.

Chapter 2:
Strategies For Selling Coins

Selling coins can be a lucrative and rewarding process, but it requires a good understanding of the market and the different strategies for selling coins effectively. The success of a coin sale depends on several elements, such as the current market conditions, the rarity and condition of the coins, and the chosen selling method. In this chapter, we will explore the different strategies for selling coins, including the pros and cons of various selling options, such as auctions, dealers, and online marketplaces. Here are some strategies for selling coins:

Timing:

Timing is a crucial factor when selling coins. Pay attention to market conditions and try to sell your coins when prices are high, and demand is strong. This may involve holding onto your coins for a period of time to allow their value to appreciate.

Selling platform:

Choose a selling platform that is appropriate for the type and value of the coins you are selling. For example, if you are selling high-value coins, you may want to consider selling through a reputable auction house or a specialized coin dealer. If you are selling lower-value coins, online marketplaces such as eBay or Amazon may be a more suitable option.

Grading and authentication:

Having your coins graded and authenticated by a reputable third-party grading service can help increase their value and make them more appealing to potential buyers.

Pricing:

Set a fair and competitive price for your coins based on market conditions and the condition and rarity of the coins. Avoid overpricing your coins, as this may deter potential buyers.

Marketing:

Develop a marketing strategy to promote your coins to potential buyers. This may include creating detailed descriptions and high-quality images of your coins, promoting them through social media or online forums, or working with a reputable dealer or auction house to reach a wider audience.

Consignment:

If you are selling high-value coins, you may want to consider consigning them to a reputable dealer or auction house. This can help ensure that your coins are marketed effectively to potential buyers and that you receive a fair price for them.

Chapter 3:
Top Websites For Coin Enthusiasts And Collectors

Th The internet has revolutionized the world of coin collecting, providing enthusiasts and collectors with a wealth of information and resources that were once difficult to access. There are now numerous websites dedicated to the world of numismatics, offering everything from educational content and forums to online marketplaces and grading services. In this chapter, we will explore the top websites for coin enthusiasts and collectors, providing an overview of the features and benefits of each site. We will cover popular websites such as the American Numismatic Association, PCGS, NGC, Heritage Auctions, and eBay, among others. Whether you are looking to expand your knowledge of coins, connect with other collectors, or buy and sell coins online, this chapter will provide you with a valuable guide to the top websites for coin enthusiasts and collectors.

PCGS Website:

The Professional Coin Grading Service (PCGS) is a top-notch coin grading service that offers resources and information on coin grading and authentication, as well as a coin price guide and coin registry.

NGC Website:

It is another popular coin grading service that offers a variety of resources and tools for collectors, including a coin price guide and coin registry.

Coin World Website:

Coin World is a weekly publication that covers news and information on the coin market, including market trends, upcoming auctions, and new coin releases.

American Numismatic Association Website:

It is a nonprofit organization created to carry out the research and collection of coins and related items. The ANA offers a variety of resources and events for collectors, including a coin price guide and a membership directory.

Heritage Auctions Website:

Heritage Auctions is a leading auction house that specializes in coins and other collectibles. The website offers information on upcoming auctions, as well as resources on coin values and market trends.

Stack's Bowers Galleries Website:

It is another popular auction house that specializes in coins, currency, and other collectibles. The website offers a range of resources and tools for collectors, including a coin price guide and online bidding for auctions.

The Red Book Website:

The Official Red Book is a guidebook for U.S. coins that provides information on coin values, mintage figures, and historical background. The book is updated annually and is a popular resource for collectors.

These websites offer a wealth of information and resources for coin enthusiasts and collectors and can be a valuable tools for staying up to date on the latest developments in the coin market.

Chapter 4:
Timing The Market For Maximum Profits

Timing is everything in the world of investing, and coin collecting is no exception. Understanding market trends and knowing when to buy and sell coins can significantly impact the returns on your investments. In this chapter, we will explore the concept of timing the market for maximum profits in coin collecting. We will discuss the various factors that affect the coin market, such as supply and demand, economic indicators, and geopolitical events. We will also examine the best times to buy and sell coins, as well as the risks and rewards associated with each. By mastering the art of timing the market, collectors, and investors can take advantage of opportunities for profit and maximize their returns. Whether you are a seasoned numismatist or a novice collector, this chapter will provide valuable insights into the timing of the coin market and how to use it to your advantage.

Research market trends:

Keep an eye on market trends and price movements for the types of coins you are looking to sell. This can help you identify the best times to sell your coins and potentially maximize your profits.

Monitor supply and demand:

Understand the supply and demand dynamics of the coin market. When there is high demand and limited supply, prices tend to go up, which can be a good time to sell. Conversely, when there is low demand and a surplus of supply, prices tend to go down, which may not be the best time to sell.

Seasonal trends:

Consider any seasonal trends in the coin market. For example, certain coins may be in higher demand during specific times of the year, such as commemorative coins around the time of the event they commemorate.

Keep an eye on economic indicators:

Economic indicators such as interest rates, inflation, and the strength of the U.S. dollar can also impact the coin market. For example, when inflation is high, precious metals like gold and silver tend to do well, which can impact the prices of coins made from those metals.

Work with an auction company or trusted dealer:

Consider working with a trusted dealer or auction company that has experience in the coin market. They can provide you with guidance on when to sell your coins and help you get the best price. Ultimately, timing the market for maximum profits requires careful research, attention to market conditions, and a bit of luck. However, by keeping these strategies in mind, you can make more informed decisions about when to sell your coins and potentially maximize your returns.

Chapter 5:
Price Guides And Pricing Tips

When it comes to buying or selling coins, determining their value is essential. Coin price guides and pricing tips serve as valuable resources in the coin-collecting world, providing collectors and dealers with insights into the value of coins. These resources typically offer price ranges for various coin types, grades, and conditions, and they can help collectors make informed decisions when buying or selling coins. In this chapter, we will explore the different types of coin price guides available, pricing tips for evaluating coins, and other useful information for navigating the world of coin collecting.

The Red Book

The Official Red Book is a guidebook for U.S. coins that have been published annually since 1946. The book is formally titled "A Guide Book of United States Coins" but is known as the Red Book because of its distinctive red cover. The Red Book provides pricing information for U.S. coins, as well as historical information and mintage figures. It also includes images and descriptions of each coin, which can be helpful for identifying coins and determining their value.

One of the unique features of the Red Book is its detailed information on the history of U.S. coins, as well as information on how to grade coins and other factors that can impact a coin's value. The book also includes a section on coin-collecting tips and advice for beginners. The Red Book is a valuable resource for collectors and investors who are interested in buying or selling U.S. coins. However, it's important to keep in mind that the prices listed in the guide are only estimates and can fluctuate based on various market conditions. Additionally, some coins may be rare or have unique characteristics that can impact their value beyond what is listed in the guide.

The Blue Book

The Handbook of United States Coins, also recognized as the Blue Book, is a popular coin price guide that has been in publication since 1942. The Blue Book is published annually and provides pricing information for U.S. coins, as well as historical information and mintage figures. The Blue Book provides pricing information for coins in various grades, as well as historical price trends and auction results. It also includes images and descriptions of each coin, which can be helpful for identifying coins and determining their value.

One of the unique features of the Blue Book is its grading section, which provides a detailed explanation of the various coin grades and how they affect a coin's value. The book also includes a section on coin-collecting tips and advice for beginners. The Blue Book is a valuable resource for collectors and investors who are interested in buying or selling U.S. coins. However, it's important to keep in mind that the prices listed in the guide are only estimates and can fluctuate based on various market conditions. Additionally, some coins may be rare or have unique characteristics that can impact their value beyond what is listed in the guide.

Coin World Coin Values

Coin World is a weekly numismatic publication that has been in circulation since 1960. They offer an online coin value guide that provides up-to-date pricing information for U.S. coins as well as world coins. The Coin World coin values guide provides pricing information for coins in various grades, as well as historical price trends and auction results. It also includes images and descriptions of each coin, which can be helpful for identifying coins and determining their value.

One of the unique features of the Coin World coin values guide is the ability to search for coins by specific criteria, such as denomination, mint mark, and date. This can be helpful for finding specific coins and determining their value based on their unique characteristics. In addition to its online coin values guide, Coin World also offers a print version that is published annually. The print version provides pricing information for U.S. coins, as well as world coins, and is a valuable resource for collectors and investors who are interested in buying or selling coins. It's important to keep in mind that the prices listed in the Coin World coin values guide are only estimates and can fluctuate based on various market conditions. Additionally, some coins may be rare or have unique characteristics that can impact their value beyond what is listed in the guide.

NGC Price Guide

The NGC Price Guide is a comprehensive online resource that provides pricing information for a wide variety of coins. The NGC (Numismatic Guaranty Corporation) is one of the top-notch coin grading services, and its price guide reflects the latest market trends and prices. The NGC Price Guide includes information on U.S. coins, world coins, and other coin-related items, such as tokens and medals. The guide provides pricing information for coins in various grades, as well as historical price trends and auction results. It also includes images and descriptions of each coin, which can be helpful for identifying coins and determining their value.

One of the unique features of the NGC Price Guide is the ability to search for coins by specific criteria, such as denomination, country, and date. This can be helpful for finding specific coins and determining their value based on their unique characteristics. The NGC Price Guide is a valuable resource for collectors and investors who are interested in buying or selling coins. However, it's important to keep in mind that the prices listed in the guide are only estimates and can fluctuate based on various market conditions. Additionally, some coins may be rare or have unique characteristics that can impact their value beyond what is listed in the guide.

PCGS Price Guide

The PCGS Price Guide is a comprehensive online resource that provides pricing information for a wide variety of coins. The PCGS (Professional Coin Grading Service) is one of the top-notch coin grading services, and its price guide reflects the latest market trends and prices. The PCGS Price Guide includes information on U.S. coins, world coins, and other coin-related items, such as tokens and medals. The guide provides pricing information for coins in various grades, as well as historical price trends and auction results. It also includes images and descriptions of each coin, which can be helpful for identifying coins and determining their value.

One of the unique features of the PCGS Price Guide is the ability to search for coins by specific criteria, such as denomination, mint mark, and grade. This can be helpful for finding specific coins and determining their value based on their unique characteristics. The PCGS Price Guide is a valuable resource for collectors and investors who are interested in buying or selling coins. However, it's important to keep in mind that the prices listed in the guide are only estimates and can fluctuate based on various market conditions. Additionally, some coins may be rare or have unique characteristics that can impact their value beyond what is listed in the guide.

Heritage Auctions Price Guide

The Heritage Auctions Price Guide is a comprehensive online resource that provides pricing information for a wide variety of coins. Heritage Auctions is one of the leading auction houses for coins and other collectibles, and its price guide reflects the latest market trends and prices. The Heritage Auctions Price Guide provides information on U.S. coins, international coins, ancient coins, and other currencies. The guide provides pricing information for coins in various grades, as well as historical price trends and auction results. It also includes images and descriptions of each coin, which can be helpful for identifying coins and determining their value. One of the unique features of the Heritage Auctions Price Guide is the ability to search for coins by auction date. This can be helpful for determining current market values based on recent auction results.

The Heritage Auctions Price Guide is a valuable resource for collectors and investors who are interested in buying or selling coins. However, it's important to keep in mind that the prices listed in the guide are only estimates and can fluctuate based on various market conditions. These price guides can be valuable resources for collectors and investors to determine the approximate value of a coin. It's important to keep in mind that the prices listed in these guides are only estimates and can fluctuate based on various market conditions.

Pricing Tips For Buying And Selling Coins:

Do your research: Before buying or selling a coin, it's important to do your research to determine its value. Use pricing guides, auction results, and other resources to get an idea of the coin's value.

- **Look for key dates and rarities**: Some coins are more valuable than others due to their rarity or historical significance. Look for key dates and rarities that can increase a coin's value.
- **Consider the coin's condition:** The condition of a coin can significantly impact its value. Look for coins that are in good condition and have been well-preserved.
- **Be aware of market conditions**: The coin market can fluctuate based on a variety of factors, such as economic conditions and supply and demand. Be aware of market conditions and adjust your pricing strategy accordingly.
- **Get multiple opinions**: If you're unsure about a coin's value, consider getting multiple opinions from reputable dealers and experts.

- Factor in transaction costs: When buying or selling coins, be sure to factor in any transaction costs, such as commissions or shipping fees, that may impact the final price.
- **Be patient:** The coin market can be slow-moving, and it may take time to find the right buyer or seller for a particular coin. Be patient, and don't rush into a transaction unless you're confident that it's the right decision.

Chapter 6:
The Coin Market Cycle

The coin market, like any other market, is subject to cycles of growth and decline. These cycles can be affected by various factors such as economic conditions, political changes, and collector trends. Understanding the coin market cycle is crucial for collectors and dealers alike, as it can help them make informed decisions about buying, selling, and collecting coins. In this chapter, we will examine the different stages of the coin market cycle and explore how collectors and dealers can navigate each stage to maximize their investments. We will also look at various indicators that can help identify where the market is in its cycle and offer strategies for success in each stage.

Introduction Stage:

In this stage, a new coin is introduced to the market, typically through a mint or dealer. The coin may generate initial interest from collectors and investors, but its value is often uncertain.

Growth Stage:

As more collectors and investors become aware of the coin, demand increases, and the price may begin to rise. This can lead to a period of growth in the market, with increasing prices and strong demand.

Maturity Stage:

At this stage, the market has reached its peak, and the coin may be in high demand from collectors and investors. Prices may remain stable or even continue to rise, but the rate of growth begins to slow.

Decline Stage:

As the market becomes saturated, demand begins to decrease, and the price may start to decline. This can lead to a period of decline in the market, with decreasing prices and weaker demand.

Bottoming Out Stage:

In this stage, the market has hit its low point, and prices may be at their lowest. However, some collectors and investors may see this as an opportunity to buy, which can help to stabilize the market.

Recovery Stage:

As the market begins to stabilize, some collectors and investors may start to buy, which can lead to a period of recovery in the market. Prices may start to rise, and demand may begin to increase once again.

It's important to note that the coin market cycle can vary depending on a variety of factors, and not all coins follow the same pattern. Additionally, different coins may be at different stages of the cycle at any given time. Understanding the coin market cycle can be helpful for collectors and investors in making informed decisions about buying and selling coins.

Chapter 7:
Navigating The Coin Dealing Industry

The coin dealing industry can be complex and challenging to navigate, whether you are a beginner or an experienced collector. With numerous dealers, auction houses, and online marketplaces, finding reliable sources and making informed decisions can be overwhelming. However, understanding the coin dealing industry's nuances and having a good strategy can help you identify the right dealers, make informed purchases, and maximize your returns. In this chapter, we will discuss the different types of dealers, how to choose the right dealer, tips for negotiating prices, and other useful information for navigating the coin dealing industry. Whether you are a seasoned collector or just starting, this chapter will provide valuable insights to help you make the most of your coin-collecting experience.

Before buying or selling coins, it's important to do your research to determine the coin's value and ensure that you're dealing with a reputable dealer. Use pricing guides, auction results, and other resources to get an idea of the coin's value, and research dealers to ensure that they have a good reputation in the industry. Coin shows are a great way to network with other collectors and dealers and learn about new coins and trends in the industry. Attending coin shows can also help you to find reputable dealers and make connections that can be helpful in the future.

Building relationships with reputable dealers can be helpful in navigating the coin dealing industry. Establishing trust with a dealer can help to ensure that you're getting fair prices and can help you to access rare coins and other opportunities. Unfortunately, the coin dealing industry is not immune to scams and fraudulent activities. Be cautious of deals that seem too good to be true, and be aware of common scams such as counterfeit coins and "pump and dump" schemes.

Professional grading services can help to authenticate coins and provide a standardized grading system to ensure that you're getting a fair price for a coin. Staying up to date on the coin market's news and trends can be helpful in making informed decisions about buying and selling coins. Subscribe to industry publications, follow industry experts on social media, and stay informed about current events that may impact the coin market.

Chapter 8:
Finding A Trusted Local Coin Dealer

Finding a trusted local coin dealer is crucial for any collector, whether you are just starting or have been collecting for years. A good dealer can provide valuable guidance and advice, offer a wide selection of coins, and ensure that you get fair prices for your purchases and sales. To find a trusted local coin dealer, start by doing your research. Check online reviews, ask for recommendations from other collectors, and attend local coin shows and auctions to meet dealers in person. When you meet a dealer, ask about their experience and qualifications, their reputation in the industry, and whether they are members of any professional associations. You should also ask about their pricing policies, return policies, and guarantees. A good dealer will be transparent and willing to answer your questions, and they should have a passion for coin collecting that shines through in their work. By taking the time to find a trusted local coin dealer, you can enjoy a more rewarding and successful coin-collecting experience.

- Ask other coin collectors or dealers for recommendations on trusted local dealers. They may be able to refer you to a reputable dealer that they have worked with in the past.
- Check online reviews of local coin dealers to see what others have to say about their experiences. Look for dealers with high ratings and positive reviews.
- Look for a dealer who is a member of a professional organization, such as the PNG or ANA. These organizations require members to adhere to strict ethical standards and can provide a level of assurance that the dealer is reputable.
- Visit the dealer in person to get a sense of their operation and to inspect the coins that they have for sale. A reputable dealer should be willing to answer your questions and provide information about the coins they are selling.
- A reputable dealer should be transparent about the coins they are selling, including the coin's grade, rarity, and price. They should also be willing to provide information about the coin's history and provenance.

- A reputable dealer may work with a professional grading service, such as PCGS or NGC, to authenticate and grade coins. Consider working with a dealer who uses these services to ensure that you're getting a fair price for a coin.

Remember, the key to finding a trusted local coin dealer is to do your research and take the time to establish a relationship with a reputable dealer who you can trust.

Chapter 9:
Mistakes To Avoid When Buying And Selling Coins

Buying and selling coins can be a rewarding and lucrative activity for collectors and dealers alike. However, it is also an industry that requires careful attention to detail, knowledge, and experience to avoid making costly mistakes. Even seasoned collectors and dealers can make mistakes that can result in significant financial losses. In this chapter, we will explore some of the most common mistakes to avoid when buying and selling coins. We will examine the importance of proper authentication and grading, the risks of overpaying or underselling, the pitfalls of speculation and hype, and other essential factors that can impact your success in the coin-collecting industry. By learning from the mistakes of others and taking the necessary precautions, you can improve your chances of success and avoid costly errors.

Failing to do your research:

One of the biggest mistakes that coin buyers and sellers make is failing to do their research. Before buying or selling a coin, it's imperative to research the coin's value, rarity, and history to ensure that you're making an informed decision.

Overpaying or underselling:

Another common mistake is overpaying for a coin or underselling it. This can happen when buyers or sellers are not aware of the current market value of a coin or fail to negotiate effectively.

Failing to authenticate coins:

Counterfeit coins are a common problem in the coin industry, and failing to authenticate a coin can lead to significant losses for buyers and sellers. Make sure to work with reputable dealers who use professional grading services to authenticate coins.

Not paying attention to grading:

The grade of a coin can significantly impact its value, so it's important to pay attention to grading when buying and selling coins. Work with reputable grading services, such as PCGS or NGC, to ensure that you're getting an accurate grade for your coins.

Selling too quickly:

Coin values can fluctuate over time, and selling too quickly can lead to missed opportunities for higher profits. Make sure to keep up to date with the current market trends and be patient when selling coins.

Failing to protect your coins:

Coins can be damaged easily, and failing to protect your coins can lead to significant losses. Make sure to store your coins in a safe and secure location and handle them carefully to prevent damage.

Not establishing a good association with a trusted dealer: Working with a reputable dealer is essential when buying and selling coins. Establishing a relationship with a trusted dealer can help you to navigate the industry and make informed decisions about buying and selling coins.

Book 6:
Discovering Rare Coins

This book is an essential resource for both beginners and seasoned collectors, offering valuable insights into the history, grading, valuation, and market trends of rare coins. With detailed descriptions, this book provides a comprehensive overview of rare coins from ancient times to modern-day issues. Whether you are a novice or an experienced collector, Discovering Rare Coins is a must-read for anyone interested in exploring the fascinating world of rare coin collecting.

Chapter 1:
Locating Rare And Valuable Coins

With so many different coins in circulation, it can be challenging to identify the ones that are truly rare and valuable. Additionally, some of the rarest coins may only be available through specialized dealers or auction houses, which can add an extra layer of complexity to the search. In this chapter, we will explore some of the most effective strategies for locating rare and valuable coins. We will cover topics such as researching and networking, attending auctions and coin shows, and building relationships with dealers and other collectors. By utilizing these strategies, collectors can increase their chances of finding rare and valuable coins and adding exciting new pieces to their collections.

Attend coin shows: Coin shows are a great place to network with other coin collectors and dealers and to see a wide range of coins. Look for shows in your area and attend them to find rare and valuable coins.

Check online auctions: Online auctions, such as eBay and Heritage Auctions, can be a great source for rare and valuable coins. Make sure to research the coins and the seller before making a purchase.

Network with other collectors: Join coin-collecting forums and groups online and in person to network with other collectors. They may be able to offer tips on where to find rare and valuable coins.

Visit local coin dealers: Local coin dealers may have rare and valuable coins in their inventory. Make sure to visit multiple dealers and establish relationships with them to increase your chances of finding rare and valuable coins.

Keep an eye out for error coins: Error coins, such as those with misprints or incorrect dates, can be rare and valuable. Keep an eye out for them when searching for coins.

Look for coins with low mintage numbers: Coins with low mintage numbers are often rare and valuable. Research the mintage numbers of specific coins to identify those with lower numbers.

Be patient: Finding rare and valuable coins can take time and patience. Be persistent in your search and keep an eye out for opportunities to acquire these coins.

Remember, when looking for rare and valuable coins, it's important to research and authenticate the coins to ensure that you're getting a fair price and a genuine coin. Work with reputable dealers and grading services to increase your chances of finding high-quality rare and valuable coins.

Chapter 2:
America's Rarest Coins

America's rarest coins are some of the most coveted and valuable items in the world of coin collecting. These coins often have a rich history and are sought after by collectors and investors alike. From colonial coins to modern-day issues, the United States has produced numerous rare and valuable coins that have captured the attention of numismatists around the globe. In this chapter, we will explore some of America's rarest coins, their history, grading, and valuation, and their significance in the coin-collecting industry.

1933 Double Eagle

It is a rare and valuable gold coin that was produced by the United States Mint. It features a portrait of Liberty statue on the obverse side and an eagle on the other, with a denomination of twenty dollars. The 1933 Double Eagle is particularly famous because none of the coins were officially released for circulation. While over 400,000 Double Eagles were minted in 1933, the United States was still during the Great Depression, and the government decided not to release any of the coins into circulation.

Although a few Double Eagles were released to collectors and dealers for numismatic purposes, the vast majority of the coins were melted down. However, a few 1933 Double Eagles were stolen from the Mint and eventually made their way into private collections. In the early 2000s, the US government attempted to reclaim one of the 1933 Double Eagles from a private collector, but the case went to court, and ultimately the collector was allowed to keep the coin. However, the US government still considers the 1933 Double Eagles to be government property, and any that are found are subject to confiscation.

1913 Liberty Head Nickel

It is one of the most famous and valuable coins in American history. Five specimens of this coin are known to exist, making it an extremely rare and highly sought-after coin. The coin was produced at the Philadelphia Mint but without authorization. It is believed that the dies for the Liberty Head design were created as a response to the release of the new Buffalo Nickel design that same year. The unauthorized dies were used to produce a small number of 1913 Liberty Head Nickels before they were discovered and destroyed.

1894-S Barber Dime

It is a rare and valuable coin that was produced at the San Francisco Mint. The coin features a portrait of Liberty on the obverse, with a wreath and the denomination on the reverse. Only 24 examples of the 1894-S Barber Dime are known to exist, making it one of the rarest coins in American numismatics. The coin's scarcity is due to a combination of factors, including low mintage numbers, a lack of demand for the denomination at the time, and the fact that many coins were likely melted down.

Because of its rarity and historical significance, the 1894-S Barber Dime is highly sought-after by collectors and investors and can command prices in the hundreds of thousands or even millions of dollars.

1804 Silver Dollar

Despite its name, the coin was not actually produced in 1804 but rather in the 1830s and 1840s as part of a special set of coins produced for diplomatic purposes. The coins were intended as gifts to foreign dignitaries, but due to a misunderstanding, the wrong date was engraved on the coins, leading to the famous 1804 Silver Dollar name. Only 15 1804 Silver Dollars are known to exist, and they are highly sought-after by collectors and investors. The coins featured a portrait of Lady Liberty on the obverse side and an eagle on the other side and were produced in proof and circulation strikes. The 1804 Silver Dollar has a long and fascinating history, with many interesting stories and legends associated with it. The coins have sold for millions of dollars at auction and are considered some of the most valuable coins in the world.

1915-S Panama-Pacific Exposition $50 Gold

It is a highly sought-after and valuable coin produced in honor of the "Panama-Pacific International Exposition," which was organized in San Francisco in 1915. The coin was designed by Robert Aitken and had a portrait of Columbia, the female personification of the USA, on the obverse side and an image of an eagle on the other side. The coin was produced in two versions, a round, and an octagonal shape, and was minted in San Francisco. Only 1,500 coins of each shape were produced, making them highly rare and valuable. The coins were sold at the Exposition for $100 each, a high price at the time, and were marketed as a way to commemorate the Exposition and support the city of San Francisco, which had recently recovered from a devastating earthquake in 1906. Today, the 1915-S Panama-Pacific Exposition $50 Gold is highly prized by collectors and investors and can command prices in the hundreds of thousands or even millions of dollars, depending on the condition and rarity of the coin.

These coins are highly prized by collectors and investors and can command prices in the millions of dollars at auction.

Chapter 3:
Rare Coins From Around The World

Rare coins from around the world offer collectors a fascinating glimpse into the diverse history, culture, and artistry of different countries and civilizations. From ancient coins that date back thousands of years to modern issues that showcase the latest technological advancements, rare coins from around the world have captured the attention of numismatists for generations. In this chapter, we will explore some of the rarest and most highly valuable coins from around the world, their historical and cultural significance, grading and valuation, and the factors that impact their value in the global coin-collecting industry.

1344 Edward III Gold "Double Leopard" Florin (England)

The 1344 Edward III Gold "Double Leopard" Florin is a very rare and valuable coin from medieval England. It is also known as the "Double Leopard" because of the two leopards on the other side of the coin. The coin was first introduced in 1344 during the reign of King Edward III of England. It was made of 23-carat gold and weighed approximately 6.98 grams. The design of the coin featured the king's portrait on the obverse side, while the other side depicted two leopards facing each other.

The "Double Leopard" Florin was one of the first gold coins to be minted in England and was intended to be used as a trade coin with continental Europe. However, it was not widely circulated and was only produced for a small period of time, making it a very rare and valuable coin. Today, the 1344 Edward III Gold "Double Leopard" Florin is highly sought after by collectors and can fetch prices in the hundreds of thousands or even millions of dollars at auction.

1992 Gold 2000 Yuan (China)

The 1992 Gold 2000 Yuan is a Chinese bullion coin that was released by the People's Republic of China. It is a 1-kilogram gold coin that has a face value of 2000 yuan. The coin was produced in both proof and uncirculated versions. The obverse side of the coin features an image of the "Hall of Prayer for Good Harvests," which is a famous temple in the Heaven complex temple in Beijing. The other side of the coin features a picture of two pandas, which is a popular symbol of China. The 1992 Gold 2000 Yuan coin is made of .999 fine gold and has a diameter of 100 mm. It was produced in limited quantities, with only 200 proof coins and 2,000 uncirculated coins minted.

Due to its rarity and large size, the 1992 Gold 2000 Yuan coin is greatly sought after by collectors and investors. It is considered a numismatic and investment-grade coin and can fetch significant premiums over its gold bullion value. The value of the coin depends on its condition, rarity, and current market demand for the coin.

1621 100 Ducats (Polish-Lithuanian Commonwealth)

The 1621 100 Ducats coin is a gold coin that was issued by the Polish-Lithuanian Commonwealth during the reign of King Sigismund III Vasa. The coin has a face value of 100 ducats and is considered one of the most valuable coins from the Commonwealth period. The obverse side of the coin features a portrait of King Sigismund III Vasa, while the other side depicts the Polish coat of arms, the crowned eagle. The coin was made of .986 fine gold and had a weight of approximately 349.2 grams, which makes it one of the heaviest gold coins in the world.

The 1621 100 Ducats coin was produced in limited quantities, with only 10 to 12 coins believed to have been minted. It was primarily intended as a gift for foreign dignitaries and as a symbol of the wealth and power of the Polish-Lithuanian Commonwealth. Today, the 1621 100 Ducats coin is highly prized by collectors and investors due to its rarity, historical significance, and high gold content. The value of the coin depends on its condition, rarity, and current market demand for the coin, but it can fetch significant sums at auction and in private sales.

2007 Queen Elizabeth II Million Dollar Coin (Canada) (Tie)

It is a special edition bullion coin minted by the Royal Canadian Mint in 2007 to commemorate Queen Elizabeth II's 60th-year rule. It is made of 99.999% pure gold and weighs 100 kilograms, with a value of $1 million CAD. The design features the portrait of Queen Elizabeth II on the obverse side and a leaf of maple on the other. The coin was created as a symbol of Canadian pride and excellence in minting, and only a few of these coins were produced.

Interestingly, the 2007 Queen Elizabeth II Million Dollar Coin was also tied with the 2010 Big Maple Leaf as the world's largest coin made out of gold until the latter somebody stole it from a museum in Berlin in 2017. Due to its rarity and value, the 2007 Queen Elizabeth II Million Dollar Coin is not intended for circulation and is primarily held as a collectible or investment. It is considered a remarkable achievement in the field of numismatics and is highly sought after by collectors around the globe.

1899 Single 9 Pond (South Africa) (Tie)

The 1899 Single 9 Pond is a rare gold coin from South Africa, which was minted in Pretoria during the Anglo-Boer War. It is called the Single nine because it features the numeral nine on the other side of the coin, representing the coin's face value of 9 pounds. The 1899 Single 9 Pond is particularly rare because only one example of this coin is known to exist. It is believed that the rest of the mintage was destroyed during the war or melted down for its gold content.

The Single 9 Pond is made of 91.67% pure gold and has a weight of 7.9881 grams. It has a diameter of 22.05mm and a thickness of 1.53mm. The obverse side of the coin had a portrait of Paul Kruger, the then President of the South African Republic, while the other side had the coat of arms of the South African Republic, with the numeral nine below it. The 1899 Single 9 Pond is considered one of the most valuable coins in the world, with an estimated value of several million US dollars. Its rarity and historical significance make it a highly sought-after collectible by numismatists and investors alike.

723 Umayyad Gold Dinar (Islamic Umayyad Kingdom)

The 723 Umayyad Gold Dinar is a historic gold coin that was minted during the reign of the Islamic Umayyad Kingdom. The Umayyad caliphate was one of the largest empires in history and ruled much of the Middle East, North Africa, and parts of Europe and Asia from 661 to 750 CE. The Umayyad Gold Dinar is made of 22-carat gold and weighs approximately 4.25 grams. It has a diameter of 20mm and a thickness of 1.4mm. The obverse side of the coin features a standing caliph holding a sword, while the other side features an inscription in Arabic script with the name of the caliph, the mint location, and the year of minting.

The 723 Umayyad Gold Dinar is particularly significant because it was minted during the reign of the Umayyad caliph Yazid II, who remained caliph from 720- 724 CE. This coin is also significant because it was minted in the city of Damascus, which was the capital of the Umayyad caliphate and a center of Islamic civilization. Due to its rarity, historical significance, and cultural importance, the 723 Umayyad Gold Dinar is a highly sought-after collectible by numismatists, historians, and investors. While its value is difficult to determine, it is known to be a valuable and prized addition to any collection of ancient coins.

2007 1 Million Canadian Gold Maple Leaf

It is a special edition "bullion" coin released by the Royal Canadian Mint in 2007. It is made of 99.999% pure gold and weighs 100 kilograms, with a value of $1 million CAD. The coin has the iconic maple leaf design on one side, while the other side has a portrait of Queen Elizabeth II. 2007 1 Million Canadian Gold Maple Leaf is considered a symbol of Canadian pride and excellence in minting.

It is also significant because it is one of the world's largest coins, with a diameter of 50cm and a thickness of 3cm. Due to its rarity and size, the coin is not intended for circulation and is primarily held as a collectible or investment. It is highly sought after by collectors and investors due to its rarity and unique size. It is considered a remarkable achievement in the field of numismatics and is a valuable addition to any collection of gold coins. While the coin's value fluctuates with the price of gold, it is generally regarded as a valuable asset due to its rarity and large size.

1368-1382 Venice, Italy Silver Grosso PCGS AU

The 1368-1382 Venice, Italy Silver Grosso is a historic silver coin that was minted during the reign of the Doge of Venice. The Venice Silver Grosso is made of 98% pure silver and weighs approximately 2.1 grams. It has a diameter of 21mm and a thickness of 0.7mm. The obverse side of this coin has the image of the Doge kneeling before Saint Mark, the patron saint of Venice, while the other side features the coat of arms of Venice.

The 1368-1382 Venice Silver Grosso is particularly significant because it was minted during the reign of Doge Andrea Contarini, who served as Doge from 1368 to 1382. This period was a time of great expansion and prosperity for Venice as the city-state grew in power and wealth through trade and conquest. The PCGS AU designation for this coin indicates that it has been graded by the Professional Coin Grading Service and is in Almost Uncirculated condition. This means that the coin has some signs of wear but still retains much of its original detail and luster.

The 1368-1382 Venice Silver Grosso is a valuable and sought-after collectible by numismatists and collectors due to its rarity, historical significance, and beautiful design. Its value can vary depending on its condition, rarity, and demand, but it is generally considered a valuable addition to any collection of historic coins.

Chapter 4:
Best Practices For Buying And Selling Rare Coins

Rare coins can be a valuable investment, but they can also be risky if proper precautions aren't taken. Whether you're buying or selling rare coins, there are a number of best practices you should follow to ensure that you're making a smart decision. Firstly, it's important to do your research. You should have a good understanding of the rare coin market, including current prices, trends, and the history of the coin you're interested in. This will help you make informed decisions about what to buy or sell and what prices are reasonable. You can find this information by reading books, attending coin shows, and talking to experienced collectors.

When buying coins, it's also imperative to only deal with trusted and reliable dealers. Look for dealers who are members of professional organizations like ANA or PNG. These organizations have strict ethical guidelines that their members must follow, and dealing with a member can provide a level of assurance that you're working with someone who is knowledgeable and trustworthy. Another important best practice when buying rare coins is to only purchase coins that are certified by a third-party grading company. These services will evaluate the coin's condition and authenticity and assign it a grade. This can help ensure that you're getting what you're paying for and that the coin is genuine.

When selling rare coins, it's important to get multiple offers and do your own research to determine a fair price. Don't be afraid to ask questions about the offers you receive, and consider factors such as the coin's rarity, condition, and historical significance. You may also want to consider working with a professional appraiser to get an objective assessment of the coin's value. It's also important to be wary of scams when buying or selling rare coins. Be cautious of deals that seem too good to be true, and don't buy or sell coins without proper documentation or certification. Additionally, never send money or coins before receiving payment or confirmation of payment. Finally, remember to take proper care of your rare coins. Store them in a cool, dry place away from sunlight, and handle them with gloves to prevent damage from oils and other substances on your hands.

Book 7:
The History Of Coin Collecting

The practice of collecting coins has a rich and fascinating history that spans back centuries, with evidence of coin collecting dating as far back as ancient Rome. Throughout the ages, coins have been valued not only for their monetary worth but also for their historical significance, artistic value, and rarity. In this chapter, we will delve into the history of coin collecting, exploring its evolution from ancient times to the modern day and examining the various factors that have contributed to its enduring appeal.

Chapter 1:
Tracing The Evolution Of Coin Collecting

Coin collecting is one of the oldest activities in the world. The advent of paper money is a relatively recent occurrence outside of China and Japan (meaning since the 18th century). Therefore, collecting notes and other forms of currency is legal, but it has a different history from that of coin collecting and is mostly contemporary. Contrary to popular belief, coin collection has been around for much longer than the Italian Renaissance, as evidenced by Emperor Augustus' appreciation for ancient and exotic coins, according to Suetonius (AD 69-122). In addition, a hoard of roughly seventy Roman gold coins found in Vidy, Switzerland, with no duplicates of the same type, suggests that the coins were collected during the time when the area was under Roman rule.

Art collecting, which has detailed and reliable records, has been a widespread practice since the third or fourth century BC. At that time, coins were widely regarded as works of art and were among the most accessible and portable objects in the art world, making it unsurprising that they were collected. Besides their function as currency, these coins were highly valued for their use in jewelry and artistic works of the era. In AD 249-251, during the reign of Trajanus Decius, the Roman Mint issued a series of coins to commemorate each of the worshipped emperors, from Augustus to Severus Alexander. These coins' designs were exact replicas of those on the honorable rulers' original coins, some of which were already close to 300 years old. It would have been difficult to categorize such an assemblage as anything other than a collection because the mint would have needed samples of the coins to serve as prototypes. Another instance of collected coins serving as an inspiration for die engravers of later age is the series of coins struck by Charlemagne in AD 805 that closely match the design and subject matter of Roman Imperial issues. Famous Italian reawakening humanist Petrarch (1304–1374) amassed an impressively aesthetic and scientific collection of antiquity coins. The artwork on the coins, which frequently depicts images of historical individuals, mythical creatures, and other subjects, appears to have been the main source of interest in numismatics during these early periods. In Asia and Africa, collecting was uncommon until very recently because these coins typically lacked imagery.

Kingly pastimes and the development of coin-collecting research:

Throughout the fifteenth and sixteenth centuries, ancient currency collecting became known as the "hobby of kings," and European monarchy predominated in the list of collectors. These benefactors also commissioned renowned painters to produce portrait or commemorative medals as well as copies of ancient coins, which later rose to valuable status. Collectors' appetites drove a small business of agents, who sought source locations for artifacts that might be sold. As would be predicted, the market's unquenchable desire led to an increase in counterfeit goods. The reason for collecting had slowly turned toward serious investigation by the 17th century. Large-scale collections were created, investigated, and cataloged as a result. During that time, numismatics developed into an academic discipline, and a number of significant treatises were published. Most importantly, thorough and widely disseminated treatises on coinage and collecting codified the flow of knowledge and new findings. During this time, the state took control of many huge private collections owned by noble families, and the following cataloging of these holdings significantly expanded our knowledge. Because this information was widely available, middle-class businesspeople and other professionals—who were both growing in number and cultural sophistication—began collecting coins as a pastime. One of the few ways the common individual might own genuine artifacts from antiquity is through collecting ancient coins, and the burgeoning collector community was aware of this. Coins are incredibly accessible artifacts from the past.

Chapter 2:
Current Practices:

During the 19th century, the network of private coin collectors grew significantly, and beginner guides started to show. The focus of coin gathering expanded from the earliest culture to modern coins, and it turned into a well-liked pastime for people. In Britain, Europe, and the US, a large number of numismatic associations were founded. Membership was available to all sexes and demographics. Coin-collecting journals began to appear, and the rising need for additional sponsors led to the development of a thriving industry. The coin-collecting association grew even more in the 20th century with the rise of coin shows, numismatic festivals, public meetings, and symposia. Some of these clubs joined hands to create significant and powerful associations. At the same time, trade associations were founded, and the professional numismatist (coin dealer) group grew closer together. A thriving coin market started to emerge at this time. Back, only the elite could afford to buy ancient coins, and there were fewer sources to get them. When the public's understanding of ancient coins as collectors broadened and a higher demand arose in the market, local business owners put in more effort to identify sources. The widespread excavation of historic sites resulted from this. Farmers also started to appreciate the value of these objects as they frequently discovered coins and other minor artifacts on their tilled fields. The cultural hubs of Europe saw the discovery, sale, and distribution of hundreds of thousands of coins.

With the development of contemporary technologies over the last 200 years, counterfeiting has become a bigger concern for collectors. False issues have existed for all time. In the past, many coins were forged, either for financial gain or out of necessity. In contrast to counterfeiting, forgery aims to sell its products in the coin collector area, where their worth as official cash is unimportant. Forgers and collectors have been engaged in a centuries-long intellectual battle.

Thankfully, the collector has access to just as many tools as the counterfeiter. The great majority of forgeries are eventually discovered. One behavior that can be linked to initial instinct is collecting. However, various coin collectors have very different methods for gathering coins. Political, economic, historical, versatile, and topical perspectives are the most prevalent. For instance, some collectors want to amass a comprehensive collection of portraits of prominent persons in either a very specific or extremely general field. Others can concentrate on the metallurgy or the connections between several denominations of an issue. Historical remembrance has always been a popular theme among collectors and coin-issuing organizations. The artistic trends of the time have been represented in coins throughout history. As a result, they offer a wide range of original sources and an excellent collection of tiny artwork to modern art students and enthusiasts. Coins offer a wide variety of subject matter from which to select and build a collection. This hobby has a vast and enduring following because of its depth and diversity of appeal levels. Much of the gathering of paper money started in the 19th century. As with any collecting, rarity raises an object's worth, but collectors may also emphasize a note's historical value. Short-lived governments (like the Confederate States of America) and short-lived historical periods (like the Russian vocation notes used in areas under Soviet control during and after World War II) all produced currency, as well as unusual currencies associated with specific historical moments (like the concentration camp money produced and used by Nazi detainees in camps like Theresienstadt during World War II).

A completely new culture of coin collectors was born with the development of the Internet. More new collectors were attracted to the hobby as a result of widespread exposure to an impressively large audience than in previous years. Both fresh opportunities and challenges resulted from this. Online buyers had a relatively low degree of experience, which led to the creation of false marketplaces that were not long-lasting. The Internet market eventually settled down after a mid-1990s excitement burst and transformed into a venue. The parallel advent of educational sites enabled a substantially faster rate of maturation among novice collectors who browse the Web. One of the major issues for online shopping sites has been regulating the integrity of sellers who pop up anonymously out of thin air on the internet. Historical coins have received more protection as coin collecting has become more widespread.

Chapter 3:
How Coin Collecting Has Shaped World History

Coins have been saved and gathered for as long as they have been struck. Coins were initially accumulated as financial security because of their intrinsic bullion worth. Nonetheless, there is proof that Roman coin collecting was done purely for interest and as a transportable kind of art. Since then, coin collecting has persisted and developed into a multi-billion dollar industry on a global scale. Even while people who collect coins are frequently called "numismatists," the term "numismatics" actually refers to the methodical study of coins and money. It is possible for someone to be both a coin collector and a numismatist or vice versa. They are frequently both! Every sort of money that is currently in circulation is referred to as currency. Coins will always be coins, even if they are no longer exchanged in monetary transactions. The Ancient Romans are one of the earliest groups of people whose coin collecting is known to have taken place.

According to Suetonius' account in De vita Caesarum, the emperor Augustus periodically distributed antiquated and unusual coins to friends and courtiers during festivals and other special occasions. During the Renaissance, coin collecting really took off. The well-known Italian philosopher Petrarch was one of the first devotees. Numerous members of the wealthy classes took up the sport. In the years that followed, many European kings, princes, and other aristocrats kept collections of ancient coins. Coin collection became known as the "Hobby of Kings" because only the very wealthy could afford it.

The Enlightenment introduced a new way of thinking that encouraged a more organized approach to collecting and studying coins. Numismatics developed into a field of study during this time, and the expanding middle class, anxious to demonstrate their newfound money, took up the hobby in order to pass the time. In the late 19th and early 20th centuries, the first coin exhibits, trade associations, and regulatory agencies were established. The first international coin collectors' conference took place in Detroit in August 1962. What was formerly known as the "Hobby of Kings" is now commonly regarded as the "King of Hobbies" since it now provides chances for enthusiasts of all ages and income levels. The market for collecting coins endures fads and crazes, just like that of all collectibles. Although the popularity of most historic coins fluctuates, these variations are typically small (for instance, the price of a Peace Dollar is, on average, somewhat lower today than it was ten years ago). Modern coinage, where limited edition items can double or triple in price in a matter of days, make fads much more obvious. Many mints impose an order limit on their most sought-after releases in an effort to deter investors and speculators. The US Mint, Royal Canadian Mint, and Royal Mint are three of the mints that provide popular collector issues the most frequently.

The appeal of the modern coin market as a whole has greatly increased as a result of several high-profile collector releases and the extensive media coverage of "modern rarities." Modern coins seem to particularly appeal to younger collectors for a variety of reasons. Modern coins are generally easier to obtain, less likely to be falsified, and affordable for individuals on a tight budget. Modern coin sets are also typically simpler to finish, which gives the collector a sense of accomplishment. While the market for modern coins has significantly increased recently, many analysts believe that the classic coin industry has, generally, slightly stagnated. This is due to a number of variables, the primary among which being the substantially greater availability of historic coins today than in earlier decades. Many of the hobbyists who sold their collections during the 2009 financial crisis to raise much-needed funds are now just growing older and passing their collections on. Analysts believe that many antique coins are undervalued as a result.

Market View:

Coin collecting tends to follow a generalized trend like most collectibles do. Even if certain issues' prices fluctuate according to fads and trends, extraordinary high-grade coins are nonetheless highly sought by collectors. As a result, the values of the world's most valuable and rare coins are rising. The United States coin market continues to be the most well-liked and valuable market by nation, a position it has held for at least the past century. Nine of the top ten most expensive coins ever are American. Canada, Australia, China, and the majority of Europe are other nations with significant coin-collecting markets. Nonetheless, practically every nation that has ever produced currency will have at least a few highly prized coins. The market for collecting coins appears to have a bright future as it remains widespread around the world. While it is true that not all coins will appreciate in value, the best approach to ensure a secure investment is to conduct the necessary research and purchase when the price and other factors are favorable. The moment to make money is not when you sell but rather when you buy; a knowledgeable collector-investor will advise you. Never let yourself be pressured into making a big purchase.

Book 8:
The Future Of Coin Collecting

As we move further into the digital age, the future of coin collecting faces a number of challenges and opportunities. In this chapter, we will explore the future of coin collection and how technology, changing societal attitudes, and evolving collector preferences may shape the hobby in the years to come. From the impact of cryptocurrencies and virtual collecting platforms to the shifting demographics of collectors, this chapter will examine the current trends and potential directions for the future of coin collecting.

Chapter 1:
A Glimpse Into The Future Of Coin Collecting

With the rise of digital currencies and the decreasing use of physical cash, the world of coin collecting is facing new challenges and opportunities. One potential avenue for the future of coin collecting is the emergence of collectible digital coins or NFTs (non-fungible tokens). These unique digital assets can be purchased and traded on blockchain platforms, allowing collectors to own rare and one-of-a-kind items. While some traditional coin collectors may balk at the idea of digital items taking the place of physical coins, others see this as an exciting new frontier for the hobby.

Another factor affecting the future of coin collecting is the growing importance of cultural and historical significance. As the world becomes more globalized and interconnected, collectors are placing greater value on coins that tell a unique story or have historical significance. This may mean that coins from lesser-known regions or time periods could become more popular as collectors seek out new and interesting pieces.

Digital coins:

As the world becomes increasingly digital, it's possible that digital coins could become a significant part of coin collecting. Digital coins, or "crypto-collectibles," are digital assets that use blockchain to verify authenticity and ownership. Some collectors are already starting to collect and trade digital coins, and it's possible that this trend could grow in the future. Increased emphasis on rarity and uniqueness: As the market for rare coins becomes more crowded, collectors may start to focus even more on finding unique or one-of-a-kind coins. This could lead to an increased emphasis on coins with interesting or unusual features, such as error coins or coins with unusual mint marks.

The growing interest in international coins:

As globalization continues to bring people and cultures closer together, it's possible that collectors will become more interested in coins from other countries. This could lead to a greater emphasis on coins with interesting designs, cultural significance, or historical importance from around the world.

Greater use of technology in coin grading:

Coin grading has traditionally been a manual and subjective process, but advancements in technology, such as machine learning and artificial intelligence, could lead to more objective and accurate grading standards. This could make it easier for collectors to identify the condition and value of their coins and could also make the grading process more efficient and cost-effective.

Overall, the future of coin collecting is likely to be shaped by a combination of technological advancements, cultural trends, and economic factors. However, no matter what changes occur, it's likely that coin collecting will continue to be a beloved hobby and a valuable way to preserve and appreciate history.

Chapter 2:
The Impact Of Technology On The Hobby

Over the past few decades, technology has revolutionized almost every aspect of our lives, and the world of coin collecting is no exception. The impact of technology on this traditional hobby has been profound, from the way collectors access and purchase coins to the tools they use to authenticate and research their collections. In this chapter, we will explore the ways in which technology has transformed coin collecting and examine some of the challenges and opportunities that lie ahead for collectors in this rapidly changing landscape.

Online marketplaces:
The rise of online marketplaces like eBay and Amazon has made it easier for collectors to buy and sell coins from anywhere in the world. This has increased the availability of rare coins and has made it easier for collectors to find the coins they need to complete their collections.

Mobile apps:
There are now mobile apps available that can help collectors manage their collections. These apps allow collectors to track the coins they have, monitor the value of their collection, and even connect with other collectors.

Online databases:
There are several online databases available that provide detailed information about coins, including their history, rarity, and value. These databases make it easier for collectors to research the coins they are interested in and make informed purchasing decisions.

Digital images:

The ability to take high-quality digital images has made it easier for collectors to examine coins in detail without having to handle them physically. This has reduced the risk of damage to valuable coins and has made it easier for collectors to share information and images with each other.

Counterfeiting:

Technology has also had an impact on coin collecting by making it easier for counterfeiters to create fake coins. However, technology has also provided collectors with new tools to help them identify counterfeit coins, including specialized software and portable scanners.

Chapter 3:
The Role Of Coin Collecting In Preserving History

Coins have been an important part of human history for thousands of years, serving not only as a medium of exchange but also as a reflection of the values, culture, and politics of the time in which they were created. As a result, coins have played a crucial role in preserving history and telling the stories of civilizations long past. In this chapter, we will examine the important role that coin collecting plays in preserving history and explore some of the ways in which collectors can use their hobby to better understand and appreciate the world around them.

Numismatic research:

Collectors and scholars use coins as historical artifacts to study the economic and political systems of past civilizations. The designs, materials, and inscriptions on coins offer insight into the social, cultural, and political values of the time in which they were first released.

Archival value:

Coins are often used to mark significant events, people, or places. Collectors and historians can use coins as primary sources to uncover information about past events or important figures. Coins are often preserved in archives and museums as valuable historical artifacts, providing a tangible connection to the past.

Conservation:

Coin collectors and numismatists play a critical role in the conservation of historical artifacts. Through their efforts to collect, preserve, and study coins, collectors and scholars help to ensure that important historical artifacts are not lost to time or destroyed by natural disasters, wars, or other catastrophes.

Education:

Coin collecting can be an educational pursuit, especially for younger generations. The study of coins can provide a unique way to teach history and culture, allowing students to see and touch the physical artifacts that represent historical events or societies.

Book 9:
Coin Collecting Around the World

The numismatic journey is a fascinating adventure that goes beyond mere coin collection. At its core, it is a pursuit of understanding. Every coin, whether old or new, carries with it tales of historical epochs, the ebb and flow of cultures, and artistic expressions that have evolved over time. Each nation imprints its unique identity, values, and heritage onto its currency, making every piece a window into its soul.

Exploring the realm of international coins is not just an endeavor of amassing a diverse collection, but also a profound journey into understanding the distinct historical, cultural, and artistic values that each nation holds dear. Just as travelers experience the thrill of discovering new lands, cultures, and traditions, coin collectors feel a similar exhilaration when they acquire a coin from a foreign land. Each coin tells a story, and every story is a chapter in the grand narrative of human civilization.

Diving deep into the world of coins from various countries is an enlightening experience. It offers insights into the socio-political events that shaped nations, the artistic movements that inspired designs, and the cultural significance behind symbols, figures, and inscriptions. Moreover, international coin collecting fosters a sense of global connectedness, making collectors appreciate the intricate web of human history and the shared values that bind us all.

In this book, we embark on a journey around the world, one coin at a time. We'll explore the rich tapestries of histories, the diverse cultures, and the mesmerizing artistry that each nation brings to the world of numismatics. Whether you're a seasoned collector or just starting, this global voyage promises to be both educational and exhilarating.

Chapter 1:
Asian Coinage: Symbols of Dynasties and Civilizations

Asia, with its sprawling landscapes and diverse cultures, has been a cradle for some of the world's earliest and most influential civilizations. The coins from this vast continent are emblematic of its rich tapestry of dynasties, kingdoms, and civilizations that have risen and fallen over millennia. Each coin stands as a testament to the might of emperors, the wisdom of sages, and the artistic prowess of its people.

Ancient Chinese Coins:

China's numismatic history is as vast and varied as its imperial lineage. The earliest Chinese coins, dating back to the Zhou Dynasty (1046–256 BCE), were cast in bronze and often had a characteristic square hole in the center, enabling them to be strung together. Designs evolved from the simple spade and knife shapes to more intricate depictions of dragons and mythical creatures under later dynasties.

The Han and Tang Dynasties saw the Silk Road's prominence, which influenced coin designs, incorporating elements from Central Asia and beyond. The subsequent dynasties continued this rich tradition, with each era producing coins that reflected its distinct cultural and artistic inclinations.

Coins of the Indian Subcontinent:

The Indian subcontinent has a numismatic history dating back to the 6th century BCE with the punch-marked silver coins used by the Mahajanapadas. The rise of the Maurya and Gupta empires saw gold coins, like the Dinara, bearing intricate designs of deities, kings, and various motifs.

The Mughal era introduced a refined coinage system with coins like the Silver Rupiya, which laid the foundation for the modern Indian Rupee. The region's diversity is well-reflected in its coinage, from the gold fanams of South India to the tribal coins of the North-East, each telling tales of opulence, spirituality, and artistry.

Japanese and Korean Coins:

Japan's coinage was heavily influenced by Chinese designs initially. The early Wado Kaichin copper coins and the subsequent gold and silver Koban coins beautifully encapsulate Japan's evolving economy and cultural shifts. Notable is the distinctive rectangular 'Kanei Tsuho' coin, widely circulated during the Edo period.

Korea, with its three kingdoms - Goguryeo, Baekje, and Silla, had its unique coinage evolution. Initial coins imitated Chinese models but soon developed Korean characteristics. By the time of the Goryeo and Joseon dynasties, Korean coin designs incorporated native script and motifs, reflecting a proud national identity.

Asian coinage is a reflection of the continent's grandeur, wisdom, and artistic brilliance. Each piece carries with it tales of emperors and sages, battles and peace treaties, and the ebb and flow of great civilizations. For a numismatist, these coins are not just metal pieces but windows into the soul of a diverse and rich continent.

Chapter 2:
African Coinage: A Glimpse of Tribal Heritage and Colonial Impact

Africa, often dubbed the cradle of humankind, has a diverse and layered history that has been encapsulated in its coinage over millennia. From the ancient civilizations of Egypt and Carthage to the tribal legacies of the Maasai and Zulu, Africa's coins tell a story of a land rich in culture, abundant in resources, and shaped by both indigenous heritage and foreign influences.

Ancient and Medieval African Coins:

The north of the continent, particularly Egypt, witnessed some of the earliest coinage in Africa. The Ptolemaic dynasty produced gold, silver, and bronze coins, bearing portraits of their rulers and intricate hieroglyphs that spoke of the pharaohs' divine connections.

Further west, the Carthaginians minted coins with depictions of their deities, hinting at the rich religious tapestry of the region. In the medieval era, the Mali Empire in West Africa introduced gold dinars, showcasing the region's immense wealth and prominence in global trade routes.

Tribal Coins and Trade Beads:

While the concept of coinage was not widespread across all African cultures, many tribes used trade beads and metal objects as currency. These items, crafted with meticulous detail, were symbols of wealth and status. In regions like the Congo, intricately made Katanga crosses made of copper were used both as a medium of exchange and as a symbol of spiritual significance.

Colonial Impact and Modern African Coinage:

The wave of colonization that swept through Africa from the 19th century onwards had a profound impact on the continent's numismatic history. European powers introduced their own currency systems, often undermining or displacing local ones. Coins minted during this period bore the portraits of European monarchs and heraldry, but over time, as colonies gained independence, new national currencies emerged. These coins began to celebrate African leaders, fauna, and symbols of cultural significance.

For instance, post-independence Ghana introduced the Cedi, featuring the likeness of its first president, Kwame Nkrumah. South Africa's Rand, while today showcasing the nation's Big Five wildlife, also serves as a reminder of the country's journey from the Apartheid era to a modern democratic nation.

Africa's coinage offers a journey through time, capturing the essence of its indigenous tribes, the grandeur of its ancient civilizations, the scars of colonization, and the hope of newly independent nations. These coins are more than mere currency; they are fragments of a vast mosaic that is the African story.

Chapter 3:
Oceanic and Island Nations: A Fusion of Culture and History

The vast expanse of Oceania, with its myriad islands and diverse cultures, has been a treasure trove of numismatic wonders. From the ancient trade shells of Papua New Guinea to the modern coins bearing the Maori designs of New Zealand, the coinage of these nations and territories reflects their unique heritage, environmental treasures, and interactions with the wider world.

Ancient and Traditional Currencies:

Long before the introduction of metal coins, the indigenous peoples of Oceania had their own systems of trade and value. In Papua New Guinea, for example, the Kina shell was not just currency but also a symbol of prestige and social status. The people of the Solomon Islands used feather money, intricate woven belts made of red feathers, considered both a currency and a work of art.

Colonial Legacies and Modern Coinage:

With the advent of European exploration and colonization, many Oceanic islands saw the introduction of foreign currencies. Coins from Britain, Spain, and France began circulating, bearing images of distant monarchs and foreign symbols. Yet, as the island nations moved towards independence and self-governance, they started to mint their own coins, fusing traditional designs with modern numismatic techniques.

Australia's coinage is a prime example, with the decimal coins introduced in 1966 featuring endemic animals such as the kangaroo, platypus, and echidna. These coins pay homage to the nation's unique wildlife while retaining the image of the British monarch on the obverse.

New Zealand's coins often feature elements of Maori culture. The one dollar coin, for instance, showcases the kiwi bird, a symbol synonymous with the nation, while other coins include representations of Maori artistry and mythology.

Pacific Island Nations: A Mosaic of Cultures:

The smaller island nations of the Pacific, like Fiji, Samoa, and Tonga, each have their unique numismatic histories. While their coins often feature native flora and fauna, they also showcase aspects of their indigenous cultures, from traditional canoes to iconic tattoos. These coins serve as both a source of national pride and a medium to educate and inform the wider world about their heritage.

Furthermore, many of these island nations have become sought-after destinations for thematic coin collectors due to their propensity to release limited edition commemorative coins, celebrating everything from local festivals to global events like the Olympics.

The coinage of Oceanic and island nations is a testament to their resilience and adaptability. While they have absorbed influences from the broader world, they have also preserved and celebrated their unique identities, crafting a numismatic narrative that is both rich in history and vibrant in its diversity.

Book 10:
Step-by-Step Guide to Getting Rich with Coin Collecting

In the vast realm of coin collecting, beyond the history, artistry, and lore, lies an enticing avenue of wealth creation. Like all investments, numismatics possesses its own unique blend of risk and reward, passion and profit. While many embark on the coin collecting journey for the sheer love of it, there's no denying the allure of its potential financial returns. But how does one traverse this intricate landscape of coin valuation, market dynamics, and economic trends to achieve tangible riches?

This book aims to bridge the gap between the passionate hobbyist and the savvy investor. Through these pages, we will explore the tools and strategies that can transform an ordinary coin collection into a formidable asset. Whether you are just starting to contemplate the financial prospects of your collection or are a seasoned collector eyeing a higher return on investment, this guide will offer insights to help you maximize your profits.

Remember, while the world of coin collecting is filled with tales of unexpected fortunes and rare finds, consistent success in this field often requires diligence, knowledge, and an astute business sense. So, let's embark on this enlightening journey, merging the thrill of collecting with the wisdom of investing, as we unveil the step-by-step guide to getting rich with coin collecting.

Chapter 1:
Building a Profitable Foundation

Navigating the numismatic realm is an intricate dance between art and science. The realm of coin collecting offers avenues both for personal gratification and financial gain. As one embarks on this journey, it is imperative to lay a solid foundation to maximize potential returns without compromising the joy and passion that often accompany this hobby. In this chapter, we will explore the dichotomy between collecting for passion and profit, understand the significance of diligent research, and emphasize the necessity of setting clear financial goals complemented by diversification.

The Potential Returns and the Art of Coin Investment

At the intersection of history, art, and commerce, coins offer an avenue for both intrinsic and monetary value. The potential returns from coins can span from modest appreciation over time to windfall gains from rare finds. However, the art of coin investment is nuanced, requiring a blend of knowledge, patience, and strategy. Factors like historical significance, rarity, condition, and market demand collectively determine a coin's value.

Collecting for Passion vs. Profit

For many, coin collecting begins as a labor of love, a personal journey through history, and an appreciation of artistry. Such collectors thrive on the stories each coin tells, the civilizations it represents, and the craftsmanship it showcases. This intrinsic value can sometimes be priceless.

On the flip side, there's an undeniable allure to the potential profits of coin collecting. With tales of rare coins fetching staggering sums at auctions, the prospect of financial gains is tantalizing. However, collecting purely for profit requires a different mindset, focused on market trends, demand-supply dynamics, and investment strategies.

Striking a balance between passion and profit can be the key to a fulfilling and lucrative numismatic journey. It's entirely possible to cultivate a collection that satiates one's soul and augments one's assets.

Research Essentials

In the world of coin investment, knowledge is the most potent currency. Delving deep into emerging markets, identifying high-value coins, and staying updated are crucial.

Emerging Markets: As economies evolve and new regions gain prominence, their coin markets can present lucrative opportunities. Staying attuned to global economic shifts can unveil new avenues for investment.

High-Value Coins: Identifying coins that have the potential for significant appreciation requires a keen understanding of rarity, historical relevance, and market demand. Engaging with expert appraisers and seasoned collectors can offer invaluable insights.

Continuous Learning: The numismatic field is ever-evolving. Subscribing to coin publications, attending seminars, and networking with other enthusiasts can help keep one's knowledge up-to-date and sharp.

Setting Clear Financial Goals and Diversification

Much like any investment, clarity of purpose is vital in coin collecting. Whether one's goal is long-term appreciation, quick profits, or leaving a legacy, having a clear roadmap can guide acquisition decisions.

Diversification, a cornerstone of investment wisdom, holds true in numismatics as well. Rather than concentrating on a single type or era of coins, spreading one's investments across various categories can mitigate risks and provide a buffer against market volatilities.

In summation, building a profitable foundation in coin collecting is a meticulous process. It intertwines the heart's passion with the mind's strategy, ensuring a rewarding journey both emotionally and financially.

Chapter 2:
Acquisition, Protection, and Growth

The world of coin collecting isn't merely about tangible assets and historical artifacts. At its core, it's an intricate web of psychological processes that drive decisions, nurture relationships, and shape the collector's journey. From the thrill of acquiring a rare piece to the security measures ensuring its protection, to the community engagement fostering growth—every step is influenced by psychological factors.

Identifying and Acquiring Key, Rare, and Historically Significant Coins

The Pursuit of Significance: The quest for rare and historically significant coins is a manifestation of our innate desire for significance. We are naturally inclined to seek out and value items that are rare or represent pivotal moments in history. This hunt stimulates dopamine, the "reward" neurotransmitter, making the chase exhilarating.

The Confirmation Bias: Collectors often gravitate towards coins that reaffirm their pre-existing beliefs or interests. Someone passionate about Roman history, for instance, might emphasize the importance of Roman coins, based on their inherent bias.

Negotiation Strategies and Building Relationships for Better Acquisitions

The Principle of Reciprocity: Humans inherently want to return favors. In negotiations, offering a goodwill gesture can pave the way for better deals. This principle is at play when collectors provide valuable insights or favors to sellers, hoping for favorable terms in return.

The Need for Affiliation: Building and maintaining relationships is rooted in our need for social connections. By forming genuine relationships with sellers, dealers, and fellow collectors, one can gain access to exclusive deals, first-hand information, and a supportive network.

Advanced Storage, Security Measures, and Insuring Your Collection

Loss Aversion: Psychologically, the pain of losing something is more potent than the pleasure of gaining. This drives collectors to invest in advanced storage and security measures. They recognize the emotional and financial impact of potential loss and prioritize the protection of their assets.

The Safety Net Mentality: Insurance provides peace of mind, anchoring a safety net for collectors. The very act of insuring their collection offers emotional comfort, knowing that even in unforeseen circumstances, their investment remains safeguarded.

Growing the Value of Your Collection through Community Engagement, Exhibitions, and Networking

The Need for Recognition: Exhibiting collections and engaging with the community feeds into the human desire for recognition and validation. Showcasing rare coins or sharing knowledge positions the collector as an authority, enhancing both their self-worth and the perceived value of their collection.

Social Proof: As collectors network and receive endorsements or validations from renowned figures in the community, their collection's perceived value grows. Social proof, a potent psychological principle, implies that if experts or a majority endorse something, it gains heightened importance and value.

In essence, the psychology behind coin collecting is as intricate and fascinating as the coins themselves. Recognizing and understanding these psychological processes can empower collectors to make more informed decisions, forge stronger connections, and enhance both the tangible and intangible value of their collections.

Chapter 3:
Maximizing Returns and Navigating Challenges

Coin collecting is not a mere hobby; for many, it's a strategic financial pursuit. To maximize returns and adeptly navigate the inherent challenges, one must understand the psychological intricacies that govern decision-making, risk assessment, and long-term planning. Let's unpack the psychology behind these vital facets of coin collecting.

The Art of Selling: Timing the Market and Leveraging Various Sales Platforms

Temporal Perception and the Fear of Missing Out (FOMO): Selling coins isn't just about knowing their value; it's about understanding the psyche of the market. Collectors often grapple with the fear of selling too early or too late. FOMO can drive premature sales, while over-attachment can lead to missed opportunities. Recognizing these emotional drivers is pivotal for timing the market adeptly.

Choice Architecture: Leveraging various platforms for sales is about catering to different audience psychologies. An online marketplace might attract a newer, tech-savvy demographic, while traditional auctions may appeal to seasoned collectors. By diversifying sales platforms, collectors tap into diverse buyer psychologies, increasing the chances of lucrative deals.

Tax Implications, Financial Management, and Understanding Market Downturns

Cognitive Dissonance: Collectors may experience discomfort when their financial actions (like selling a prized coin) conflict with their internal values or knowledge (understanding its potential future value). This psychological tension necessitates robust financial management to balance immediate gains against future potential.

Loss Aversion and Market Downturns: Collectors, like all investors, dread market downturns. The psychological pain of potential loss can sometimes overshadow rational decision-making. Successful collectors learn to view downturns with perspective, understanding them as cyclical and inevitable, rather than catastrophically final.

Recognizing and Avoiding Pitfalls that Impact Profitability

Confirmation Bias: This cognitive shortcut can be a pitfall. Collectors might seek out information that validates their existing beliefs, leading to tunnel vision. For instance, if they believe a certain coin will rise in value, they may ignore contradictory market indicators, impacting profitability.

Overconfidence: A collector's past successes can lead to overconfidence, making them prone to underestimate risks. Recognizing this bias ensures a continuous, grounded assessment of decisions and their potential outcomes.

Strategic Planning for Long-term Wealth Generation and Leaving a Legacy

Future Self-Continuity: This psychological concept pertains to the connection individuals feel with their future selves. Collectors who identify closely with their future selves are more likely to engage in long-term strategic planning, ensuring the generation of wealth extends beyond their immediate needs.

Legacy and the Need for Transcendence: The desire to leave behind a legacy stems from the human need for transcendence and immortality. Coin collectors, especially those with rare or historically significant pieces, often view their collection as an extension of their life's work and identity. Thus, planning for legacy becomes not just a financial strategy, but a deeply personal endeavor.

In sum, the path to maximizing returns and skirting challenges in coin collecting is laden with psychological nuances. Harnessing a keen understanding of these subtleties allows collectors to make informed, strategic decisions, balancing passion with pragmatism, and ensuring both personal and financial fulfillment.

Conclusion

With a little bit of knowledge and patience, beginners can quickly become adept at identifying and acquiring coins, building a collection that is both valuable and personally meaningful. As you continue to explore the world of coin collecting, remember to approach the hobby with an open mind and a willingness to learn. Whether you're interested in ancient coins, modern commemoratives, or something in between, there is always more to discover and appreciate. So go ahead and start your collection today - you never know where the journey will take you!

Regards

Dear reader,

Thank you for taking the time to read this and for coming to the conclusion of this book.

Your commitment means more to me than words can express as it gives life to my words and I am deeply grateful to you.

If this reading has satisfied and helped you, I would be deeply grateful if you would take a moment of your time to leave a review on Amazon.

Such feedback is invaluable, it helps other readers discover this work and gives me inspiration to continue to improve my work as a writer.

Thank you with all my heart.

Made in United States
North Haven, CT
05 September 2023